A NEW BEGINNING

A NEW BEGINNING

VALENTINA REXHAJ

A NEW BEGINNING
Valentina Rexhaj
Editor: Anife Kasa
Translation: Ridvan Bunjaku
Concept, Design, and Cover Illustration: Halil Xhafa

Printed in United States of America

ISBN Paperback 978-1-988680-90-3
ISBN Hardcopy 978-1-988680-91-0
ISBN Digital 978-1-988680-92-7

First Edition, 2025

To my three beloved sons,
the eternal source of my love and inspiration.

And to every child, every dreamer, and every seeker across the world
who is ready to awaken,
to break free from the illusions of limitation,
and to remember the immeasurable power that lives within.

This book is a call to your soul—
to rise, to create, and to embrace
a new beginning.

May these pages remind you that you are the author of your destiny,
the creator of your reality,
and that the life you long for
is already waiting for you to claim it.

TABLE OF CONTENTS

Introduction

I am profoundly grateful and overjoyed to present this book – a true reflection of the knowledge, experiences, and wisdom I have gathered along my life's journey. It fills me with immense happiness to know that this work has found its way into your hands. As you turn these pages, I hope it inspires, uplifts, and resonates with you on a deeply personal level, marking the beginning of something extraordinary in your own story. To those who have walked alongside me and those I have been fortunate enough to touch, I am deeply grateful. Without you, this book might have remained just a dream. You inspire me every day and serve as a reflection of how much I love what I do. We are deeply connected through the essence of who we are, and this book is a manifestation of us. I wrote this book in the comfort of my home and office, but also in the serene embrace of nature, by the Limmat River in Switzerland. It was here that I spent a considerable amount of time during difficult periods. I have come to regard this place as magical. It was here that I immersed myself in meditation, attuning to the gentle murmur of the river, the symphony of birdsong, and the caress of the breeze. In this sacred space, I cultivated mindfulness, grounding myself in the present moment - the now - where life, in its purest form, unfolds.

I wrote most of this book in my office, where, after meditation, I found myself receiving inspiration from within. In the stillness of that space, away from external distractions, I felt a deep sense of calm and joy. It was in those quiet moments, alone with my inner voice, that the words flowed effortlessly, each one a reflection of the clarity I had cultivated through mindfulness and introspection. There were times when inspiration didn't come as easily as I had hoped. Several times, as I sat down to write, I realized that I wasn't able to express what I truly wanted to convey. In those moments, I chose to stop, recognizing that writing must come from a place of clarity and purpose. As a result, it took me over a year to complete this book, during which I incorporated concepts and methods learned from seminars, academies, and the many books I have read. These teachings have played a crucial role in transforming the quality of my life. In writing this, I have shared all that I know.

However, it is not enough simply to read this book- you must engage with it and embody its lessons. While books enrich us with knowledge, true transformation occurs only when we apply what we learn. When you incorporate the wisdom from these pages into your daily life and share it with others, you've achieved the essence of this work. Otherwise, it remains just a text to be read.

This book is written with simplicity and clarity, yet it serves as a powerful catalyst for a new beginning. Every day presents an opportunity to live more fully, to connect with those we love, and to embrace the potential within us.

I dedicate this book to you because I know that the world is filled with good people. I hope that, through your light, you will contribute positively to the world. Everything you need is already inside you; this book is merely a guide to help you unfold and start using what you already possess. Everything comes to you at the right time, at the right moment. At the beginning of my spiritual journey, I made a promise to myself: I would not leave this world without making a positive impact. That change began within me because, by transforming yourself, you transform the world. By serving life with the unique gift you have, you, too, have the power to make a difference. You are a gift to the world.

CHAPTER

EAGLE OR SHELL

When God created the world, He began by bringing forth all living beings. Initially, He created a shell, destined to lead a monotonous and uneventful existence. Its daily routine consisted of filtering water, endlessly opening and closing its mouth -a continuous cycle of repetition and simplicity. Then God created the eagle, with such grace and strength. Granting freedom and wings to soar across mountains, seas, plains, and valleys. He gave it the power to rule the skies and other birds, yet also entrusted it with the responsibility of nurturing and protecting its young. Subsequently, God created man. He brought him to the shell, which opened and closed its mouth several times, doing nothing else. He then led him to the eagle, which soared freely in the blue sky, nurturing and safeguarding its young from danger. Man was faced with the decision of which life he wished to lead. In truth, we are all confronted with the same profound decision: will we choose the life of the shell or that of the eagle?

(An Old Indian Story)

I began this book with this story because it deeply inspired me a few years ago. It prompted me to reflect on my own life and evaluate the kind of life I was living. I questioned whether I was merely repeating the same actions day after day, thereby creating a monotonous existence like the shell, or if I was embracing the freedom of the eagle – stepping out of my comfort zone and actively shaping the life I desired. The story encouraged me to learn, discover new things every day, and grow as an individual, striving to become the best version of myself.

From the moment I began making different decisions to change my habits and beliefs, I gradually discovered that the reality I had been living was likely just one of many possible realities. I was in that reality because I wasn't taking any action to change – it was simply the result of repeating the same patterns. To create a different reality, we must choose to be like the eagle, not the shell. This story has had a profound impact on me, and I am excited that this book will serve as another source of inspiration for you.

We have the freedom to choose whether we want to live the life of the shell, symbolizing those who resist growth and prefer to maintain their ordinary, unchanging lives. These individuals, like caterpillars, live without purpose other than to exist. Caterpillars do not seek meaning in life; they simply wish to live. However, we are miracles in our own right, possessing far more potential than we often realize, with an unlimited capacity to grow and evolve. Throughout this journey, I hear stories daily from individuals who have transformed themselves by recognizing the power within them and taking responsibility for their lives. With this book, you will have the opportunity to help yourself or others by instilling a newfound sense of confidence and conviction—something unlike what you may have experienced thus far. Together, we can reveal a different perspective, one that challenges the fear-based image we are often conditioned to see. This shift will empower us to find greater courage within ourselves and overcome the limitations that fear imposes.

This book will guide you in overcoming life's challenges by fostering the belief that you can succeed, and that, if you believe, nothing is impossible. Whether it's overcoming various illnesses, changing your reality, attracting the things you love, or experiencing the miracles that unfold each day by harnessing the power within you, this book has been a gift in my life and will undoubtedly be one in the lives of all who read it. Life is not defined by what happens to us, but by how we perceive what happens. This means that, throughout life, we will face events that may not initially seem favorable, but every challenge that we label as such carries a message and offers a lesson. It is like a letter containing wisdom, and if we do not open it to learn from it, life will send that same letter again and again until we understand its purpose. Many ailments are closely linked to our negative emotions. Modern science has supported this idea, showing that diseases often stem from a lack of harmony with nature. Our thoughts and feelings have a direct impact on our cells, meaning we can inadvertently make our bodies sick with negative thoughts. Likewise, while healthy food plays a vital role in our well-being, if consumed with negative thoughts, it loses much of its beneficial effect. You may know individuals who diligently care for their bodies, eating healthy but doing so out of fear. Though they are mindful of their diet, this fear ultimately harms their overall well-being.

It harms them much more than if they were to simply focus on eating healthy without being overly meticulous, while also prioritizing fruits, vegetables, minerals, and proper oils for the body, as well as being mindful of their thoughts and emotions. It is not a new concept that people have healed their bodies and performed miracles. If we approach things purely through logic, we may not get very far, as logic alone is limited. It is imagination that has enabled many individuals to change their reality. Take, for example, my friend Bekim, who, despite being told by doctors that he would never walk again and would remain immobile for the rest of his life, visualized himself walking every day. After several months, what he had first imagined became a reality. Bekim is not alone in his success. Many others, who for years relied on medications for conditions such as high blood pressure, heart issues, and various other ailments, have healed themselves through visualization and now enjoy good health. I had the privilege of working with a person who, with the help of guided meditations, advice from myself and others, and daily practice, was able to stop taking drugs. By doing so, he cleansed his body and freed himself from the hold of addiction.

We are undergoing a transformative process where a new energy is emerging. People from all corners of the world are being called to change, to awaken. Like many others, I had lost touch with my intuition and lived as though the material world were the only reality. The beliefs and convictions I held shaped my experiences, and life simply validated them. I lived as if I were a victim of circumstances, accepting this as my fate. True life will begin—or, more accurately, we will truly begin to live—when we are willing to connect with the great intelligence, which we call God, and allow this creative energy to flow through us. When we connect with spiritual energy, we realize that we are inherently creative and must take responsibility for the reality we create. We will come to understand that this creative energy has always resided within us. Over the years, as I invested in myself, I have been fascinated by how many people have transformed their realities simply by changing their beliefs. Once I began to change my own beliefs, I became aware of what I was carrying within me. The desire to see people awaken from their long slumber continues to inspire me daily. I find joy when people begin to tap into their inner power, when they realize that they are far more powerful than they had ever believed. They start using the positive energy they never knew they possessed. This power is within all of us, even though many of us walk through life feeling incapable, with our heads down.

Many of us walk through life thinking that we are nothing, worthless, and powerless. No matter what your past may hold, or what you have been told and accepted as truth, this book has come into your hands for a reason. It is here to remind you that you possess the power to transform yourself and create the personality you desire, even if your mind continues to repeat the messages you've heard all your life. Think of it like a movie. Until now, you may not have been the director. In fact, you were, but you allowed others to take the reins of your story. Now, you are the director, and you have the power to shape your life as you wish. We are the creators of our reality and can manifest whatever experiences we desire. It may sound unusual, but it is undeniably true. This book will provide you with deeper insights into your soul, mind, and body. The more we learn to flow with the current of life, listen to our intuition, and work with our emotions, the more vital energy will enter our lives. Living in the light not only benefits us but also positively impacts those around us. You will make a difference in the world. If you wish to change the world, start by changing yourself. By transforming yourself, you are already in the process of changing the world. By stepping into your own power, you allow others to do the same, igniting their own light.

You are likse a lantern, and with your light, you can illuminate the path for many others. The more you embrace who you truly are, love yourself, and appreciate life, the more self-confidence you will gain. As you change, others will begin to behave differently toward you—not because they have changed, but because you have altered the energy around you. They will interact with you in the way you treat yourself. Everything outside of you reflects your inner world, and this truth will open your eyes, encouraging you to look inward and make improvements there. As Mahatma Gandhi wisely said, 'Be the change you wish to see in the world.' As we evolve within, everything around us changes. To understand more about the mind, I would like to explain why many people end up repeating the same experiences in their lives and why they only perceive the reality they currently inhabit. In the first book, I discussed the Law of Attraction, and I will revise some key points. Whether we believe in something or not, we will receive proof of it. If we don't believe, we will still receive confirmation that our beliefs are true

Chapter

As Within, So Without

If the outside world is a reflection of what I carry inside, then this is valuable information, as it allows me to identify what I don't like and take the opportunity to change it. The mirror of the external world reveals what lies deep within us. Everything I create externally, and everything I dislike, is a reflection of my inner beliefs. All the people I encounter represent different aspects and emotions that reflect my inner self. Everything that happens in my life is a gift, designed to help raise my awareness. I have learned to view life as a continuous learning process, and the external world acts as a mirror to facilitate this. It shows me the aspects I carry within myself. If the 'movie' of my life is centered around conflict, I must turn inward to explore what I am fighting within myself. This mirror also reflects my life when I trust myself and remain authentic. When I am true to myself, everything falls into place, and life flows with a sense of ease—almost like a miracle. I am grateful that not everything has turned out as planned, for life would lose its intrigue if I were entirely enlightened and wise.

Life is still teaching me, and I grow every day. I learn, meditate, and reflect on myself. Life is a beautiful journey full of gifts, though often these gifts don't seem pleasant at first. We may resist them, but they are exactly what we need to rise and reach a higher level of consciousness. Others help me complete the experiences I am here to try and test. Education teaches us to live the life we desire, but it is through life experiences—what we learn from contrasts—that we gain wisdom. Everything that happens in our lives happens for us, not against us. It depends on how we choose to perceive these experiences and whether we are open to receiving the messages they carry. Nature is always at our service. It brings us the same lessons until we learn them. Therefore, the things we see outside—whether we like them or not—are a reflection of our inner world. They mirror the programs and filters we have created for life. When I began to notice how the outside world mirrored my inner state, I was often amazed at how this was possible. For example, I might see beggars on the street, and at first, I wondered how this could be a reflection of me. But I realized it wasn't about how people behave externally, but rather about how I perceive them. It's about the emotions they evoke in me. Do I have any prejudices or negative feelings toward them? Why do I feel this way? Who has influenced me to adopt these prejudices? These feelings have been ingrained in my body from various life experiences. I have internalized them, and I have created emotions related to those situations. Just as I have created those emotions in response to experiences, I also interpret and feel them from the outside world. Entering into stillness has helped me gain clarity and insight into these patterns.

By observing my thoughts and emotions, I have begun to connect with aspects of myself that I had long ignored. Whenever I felt a negative emotion triggered by an external event or someone else's actions, I resisted the urge to criticize or blame either the external world or myself. Instead, I paused and asked myself why I felt that way and reflected on my thoughts about the situation. The external world acts as a mirror, reflecting back to us what we hold inside. Each event or interaction is like a letter carrying a message—a lesson meant to reveal what lies within us. This realization marked the beginning of my transformation: by using these reflections to better understand myself. I acknowledge that this process is not as simple as it may sound. However, when you take full responsibility for your life and understand that you are the creator of your experience, this realization becomes liberating. Transformation begins when you return to yourself, accept the emotions and pains you carry, and actively choose to reshape them with thoughts that align with the life you desire. Many of us unconsciously create from old programming, making us feel like victims of fate or circumstances. While we may not always influence external events, we do have the power to decide how we feel and how we react to them. The mirror of life has been a powerful tool for me, though it was difficult at first. My ego resisted, flaring up at the idea that what I saw in others was a reflection of myself. When negative emotions surfaced, it was hard to admit that they stemmed from me—that the way I perceived others was a projection of my inner world. Walking the path toward your true self is not easy.

There will be times when you take a few steps back, and that's okay. What matters is that you don't give up until you become the person you aspire to be. To reach the core of who you truly are, you must first clear away everything you are not. You need to embrace and experience the full range of human emotions to uncover the profound love within yourself. This is the journey of the soul, which has come to test and learn from the opposites within you. Nothing outside will change until you transform what is within. Reflect on how happy you feel in life—it reveals your thoughts about yourself, your life, and others. Examine what kind of friend you are, and you will see how it mirrors the kind of company you keep. Consider what kind of partner you are, your beliefs about relationships, and your expectations—this too will reflect back at you through your experiences. Think about your thoughts and emotions regarding money—your beliefs about abundance or lack—and observe how the world mirrors those inner perspectives. The outside world is simply a reflection of the beliefs, emotions, and attitudes you carry within yourself.

CHAPTER

AS WITHOUT, SO WITHIN

Although we create from the inside out, the experiences we encounter daily exert a significant influence on our lives. We live in an era characterized by constant exposure to external information, much of which is negative in nature. We engage with individuals who complain, adopt a victim mentality, and focus predominantly on the challenges and hardships of life. Our brains contain mirror neurons, which enable us to mimic the behaviors, language, and attitudes of those around us, thereby shaping our own self-perception. Over time, these external influences—habits, behaviors, and thought patterns—become deeply ingrained in our identity.

However, we should not isolate ourselves entirely from individuals who may embody negativity, as some may be seeking personal transformation and growth. They, too, are on their path to self-awareness and change. From childhood, we are conditioned by the beliefs of our parents, social circles, and broader societal influences. Yet, in today's world, we possess the invaluable opportunity to pursue knowledge and connect with individuals of higher consciousness and success through books, YouTube, and various social platforms.

Upon gaining a deeper understanding of the mind's workings and the profound impact of our environment, I became more intentional in selecting the company I kept. Initially, I chose to engage with these individuals virtually—listening to them, learning from them, and reshaping my own beliefs. This conscious shift enabled me to evolve and act in alignment with a higher level of consciousness. I am the one who, at the moment I comprehended the workings of the mind and the significance of our surroundings—what we expose ourselves to and who we choose to associate with—made a deliberate choice to surround myself with them, albeit virtually at first. I listened to them, learned from them, and adapted, allowing my beliefs to evolve and my actions to mirror theirs. Consequently, my reality shifted accordingly.

After many years of investing in my personal growth, I can confidently assert that I have undergone a significant transformation. My current reality serves as a testament to this change, as I have altered the way I think, the way I feel, and, ultimately, the trajectory of my life.

You Are the Average of the Five People You Spend the Most Time With

Take a moment to reflect on the people you spend time with. Even if you study and read, you may not notice significant changes in your life right away. Ask yourself: Are these people role models for you? Do you aspire to have what they have, or to live the way they live? Imagine yourself standing on a table, trying to climb higher. One person is lifting you up while another is pulling you down. Who do you think will prevail? Of course, the person pulling you down will likely succeed in dragging you off the table.

Now, ask yourself how you feel after spending time with these people:

- Do you feel better?
- Do you feel richer (in terms of positive ideas and thoughts)?
- Do you feel motivated and energized after being around them?

I consider it important to ask myself these questions because we tend to become what we think about ourselves. Often, these thoughts are not our own, but rather what we absorb from others, and many times, these influences are not in our favor. By repeatedly hearing, internalizing, and seeking experiences related to these external thoughts, they eventually become beliefs, shaping the way we live.

For a period, when I struggled to manage my emotions, the words of others had a significant influence on me. I made a conscious decision to distance myself from people whose lives or attitudes I did not want to emulate. I no longer wished to associate with them.Over time, life has taught me that some of the individuals I allow into my life are also those who operate at a lower vibration. About a third of the people I interact with are at a low vibration because, at one point, I was one of them. Someone helped me rise, and now, I help others rise as well. They need this support, and they seek my presence so that I can remind them of their own inner power. True greatness emerges when we help others recognize their own greatness, not by showcasing our own. A person becomes great by assisting and serving others, helping them realize their potential. This is my mission—to help as many people as possible appreciate their own value and embrace the power that resides within them. I am referring to those who are open to receiving love, those who are ready to listen. When they are ready, they will hear you; otherwise, your words will hold no meaning. Those who seek only to consume your precious time, speaking incessantly, complaining, and portraying themselves as victims, ultimately drain your energy. Their primary desire is attention, and they continue to perceive you as they always have. Now, ask yourself: Do you truly wish to squander your valuable time on individuals who are neither open to receiving nor willing to listen to what you have to offer? The majority live comfortably, yet the ones who truly matter—those who embrace different perspectives and navigate life uniquely—are the individuals of elevated consciousness. They do not conform to the crowd. They require less because they have chosen a path of independence, actively shaping their own reality. They have assumed full responsibility for their lives, refusing to adopt a victim mentality. As creators of their own existence, they embody true freedom. Society may label them as unconventional, even eccentric, but let me ask you this: Would you rather be considered "normal" or be seen as unconventional and genuinely happy? If you choose to separate yourself from the masses, to stand out, you may be deemed “crazy” by conventional standards. Yet, those who break away from societal norms do not concern themselves with public opinion, for they have witnessed firsthand the power of crafting their own reality. And do not underestimate the impact of this journey—it has transformed not only my mindset but also my outward presence. Through reading about these extraordinary individuals, attending numerous seminars, immersing myself in books, and consuming thousands of insightful videos, I continue to evolve, educate myself, and gain new wisdom daily. My life has taken on a profound new quality, and I am deeply grateful to have embarked on this transformative journey.

Time is our most valuable asset, as our existence on this planet is finite. The biological clock is neither limitless nor sufficient. Each passing day is one less day ahead. Every moment lost is a moment subtracted from our lives. Instead of wasting time on criticism, invest it in self-improvement. Treasure your time—it is given to you freely, yet it is priceless. Time is like a diamond that cannot be bought or sold. We may be aware of when our journey begins, but we remain uncertain about when it will end. Death is inevitable, yet its timing is unknown. Life is like a pile of bricks before us. With each passing day, we take a brick from the pile and discard it, reducing what remains. Whether our lives amount to a mere scattered heap or a well-constructed fortress depends on how we choose to use each brick. When I came to this realization—having wasted time on TV series and trivial distractions that only brought me discontent—I chose to honor time, cherish each moment, and devote myself to experiences that enrich my life. I became intentional about living in the present, ensuring that time did not slip away unnoticed. Many of us merely exist, passing through life as if entering one door and leaving through another without truly experiencing it. That is why I prioritize mindfulness, education, and authenticity—to cultivate self-respect, gratitude, and a deep appreciation for every moment I am given.

I live, I am alive, I breathe—I am present in life, connected to everything that exists. Isn't that reason enough to be grateful? Recognize the power of words, for they hold profound influence. I made it a habit to draw inspiration from enlightened individuals, those of elevated consciousness, and this practice became an integral part of my daily life. I want to show you that what you engage with shapes your world, your life, your reality. Our thoughts generate emotions, and emotions drive actions. Actions, in turn, create results, and ultimately, our results define us. They serve as our CV, our biography—the legacy we leave behind.

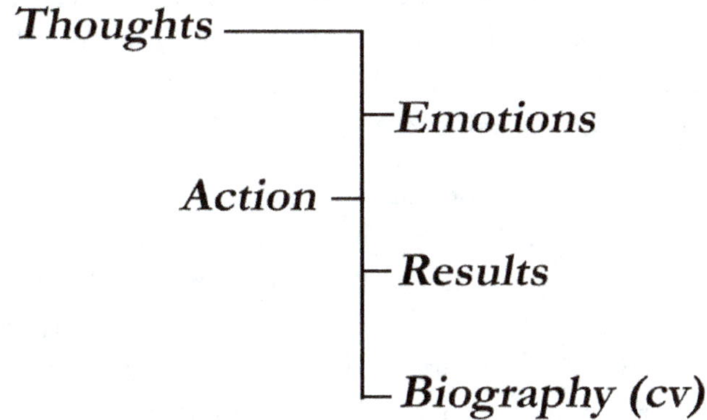

Our thoughts and actions today stem from the unconscious patterns we hold. Thoughts give rise to emotions, and our emotional state also shapes our thoughts. The most effective way to transform deeply ingrained beliefs is through a trance state, achieved through meditation or hypnosis, where the critical mind steps aside, allowing for profound internal change.

How do we best absorb lessons, and how do they become embedded in our subconscious mind? Recent research indicates that the more senses we engage, the more effective the learning process becomes. Studies suggest that the way we internalize knowledge varies depending on the sensory input involved, with the following effectiveness rates:

- 20% through listening alone
- 30% through watching alone
- 45% by combining listening and watching
- 70% by incorporating listening, watching, and repetition
- 92% when we integrate listening, watching, repetition, and emotional experiences—essentially, when we are fully present in the moment.

Everything feels challenging at first, uncertain in the middle, but rewarding in the end. Consider a child learning to walk. Though unsteady at first and falling multiple times, they persistently rise and try again.

Through repeated efforts, they gradually gain balance and eventually walk with ease. Success does not come from a single attempt but from continuous perseverance. The child has one clear goal—to walk—and through determination, they achieve it.

Every transformation in life demands energy, much like a spaceship requires immense power to launch. The greatest effort is needed at the beginning, where most of the fuel is consumed. However, once momentum is gained, the journey becomes smoother, requiring significantly less energy to maintain its course—just as a spaceship effortlessly orbits the Earth after breaking through the atmosphere. To create changes in life, it is essential to transform the way we think and feel. Any deviation from our subconscious patterns requires energy, as the subconscious stores information in a way that conserves energy, allowing us to perform actions automatically. How beautifully nature has orchestrated everything—so wonderfully and perfectly. However, if we did not experience an ideal childhood or were raised by parents who were neither affluent nor content, most of us, influenced by the programs within us, unconsciously tend to recreate similar realities. Through conscious awareness, we possess the power to change these patterns. We achieve this by altering our mindset and attitude. When I realized this, I began practicing affirmations and integrating the teachings of others. But I want to emphasize that you must remain open to learning from others. Do not approach life with the mindset that you are already a "full glass" and assume that you know everything. If you believe you have acquired sufficient knowledge or merely gathered information, take an honest look at your life. Your reality—your reflection in the mirror—reveals whether you are truly fulfilled in all areas of your life. Therefore, be honest with yourself.

"If you wish to be successful, there is one fundamental rule: Never lie to yourself." – Paulo Coelho

One day, when I was lost and didn't know where the way out was, I did exactly what I felt needed to be done at that moment. I went to the mirror, looked myself in the eyes, and said out loud to myself, "Admit that you don't know, because if you had known, you would be healthy and happy now, but you don't have either." And there, I lowered my ego, which thought it knew better than everyone, always wanted to be right, and have everything under control. I was honest with myself; I opened my mind and heart to trust those who had finally managed to be fulfilled in their lives and be happy. By adopting their habits, listening, learning, and reading their thoughts, I became aware of their beliefs and made them mine, changing the vibration of my body to attract differently, thus changing my reality. I can say that my life has changed drastically. I have worked hard with all that you will now find in this book, and it's not that I understood everything from the beginning. There is still a lot to understand on this journey. It's nice when, every day, I hear something new—something I've never heard before—and it fits inside me just the way I need it at that moment. With the beautiful journey you've taken, you will enrich your life. Do not criticize yourself if the change does not come soon. Everything will be fine because the frequencies of your brain must change to be in sync with the information you receive, so embrace it. Remember the saying: **"Everything comes at its right time."**

Nourish yourself from the outside with what will change your life for the better, so that you can have inner peace, be in harmony with yourself, and live in love. Be thankful for every person, every experience, and every emotion that has brought you here today because life calls us; the heart, with every beat, wants to remind you of who you are. Be thankful for everything you have. Not all happy people are grateful, but those who are thankful are happy! Don't live a day without gratitude. He who is thankful for what he has has no time to complain about what he does not have.

A 92-year-old man, after the death of his wife, decided to go to the nursing home. The accommodation was large for him, and he was still strong and eager to socialize with other people. In the nursing home, he waited for a while in the corridor while they prepared the room where he would stay. A young man approached him and told him that the room was ready. He thanked him and smiled at the young boy while holding onto a cane. Before entering the elevator, the old man looked around and said, "I like the room!" The young man was surprised to hear the old man say that when he hadn't yet seen the room where he would stay. With curiosity, he asked, "How is it possible that you like the room without seeing it yet?" The old man looked at him with wisdom and said: "Whether I like the room or not does not depend on how you have arranged it, but on my perception and from the perspective through which I will view it. And I have decided to be happy. I make this decision every day because I can choose. I can lie down and think about what is going wrong or what I can't do, or I can be thankful for what I still can do. Every day is a gift to us, and as long as I open my eyes, I want to enjoy the day. And as long as I can open my mouth, I want to thank God for all the happy hours I've lived and all those I am living.

CHAPTER

GRATTITUDE IS A CHOUCE YOU MAKE

Gratitude is a profound feeling that brings a sense of fulfillment, satisfaction, and heightened awareness. It arises from recognizing and appreciating the things we have in our lives. I do not want this book to overlook what is truly important. My goal is to articulate the most powerful method for inviting joy and transformation into your life.

Many years ago, I failed to recognize how much I lacked within myself. Everything I possessed—breath, sight, hearing, voice, movement, a smile, companionship, children's laughter, food, water, the love of family, and much more—I perceived as ordinary and unremarkable. However, there is no more powerful method for inviting joy into your life and transforming your energy than gratitude.

When you express gratitude, you train yourself to recognize and appreciate the good things you have now, as well as those you will receive in the future. Prejudices dissipate when gratitude takes hold. When gratitude envelops you, peace flows through your being, leaving no space for negativity. You align with the beautiful energy within you, and your mind becomes receptive to the wisdom you carry. Gratitude serves as an antidote to unhappiness, effortlessly transforming negativity into positivity. When you face the sun, you do not see the shadow; when you turn toward the shadow, you do not see the sun. Gratitude brings lightness, humor, relaxation, and inner peace. As Melody Beattie once said: *"Gratitude makes sense of our past, brings peace for today, and creates a vision for tomorrow."*

Gratitude can indeed change your life. Over time, by focusing on the good things you have, you train yourself to see them more clearly. This, in turn, brings fulfillment and ease, making you more attractive—something you will eventually be thankful for. As with all aspects of life, universal laws play a role: like attracts like. If you are ungrateful and instead complain about what you lack, you will live in scarcity. You will attract situations and circumstances where even the things you have may slip away because your focus is on what is missing rather than on appreciating the present moment. Everything you dream of having already exists. By changing your energy—the way you vibrate—you attract those things into your life.

> ***"For everyone who has will be given more, and he will have an abundance. But the one who does not have, even what he has will be taken away from him."*** *—Matthew*

This saying carries deep significance. Those who dwell in lack will continue to experience it, as like attracts like. Those who express gratitude signal to the universe that they already possess abundance. By giving thanks, they align with the energy of abundance rather than scarcity, thereby attracting even more into their lives. Gratitude creates a sense of completeness, leading to further abundance. I understand that it may not be easy to feel thankful when you feel you have nothing to be grateful for. But consider this: if you believe you have nothing to be thankful for, you are mistaken. Even if you spent your last money to buy this book, if you haven't had enough food for the entire week, or if you lost something important in your life, there is always something to be grateful for.

If, starting today, you make it a habit to return to yourself—to thank the air, the sun, and your body for everything it does for you without effort, for the miracle of life—your life will transform through gratitude. As I have mentioned in this book, gratitude is a practice that takes time to develop. Teaching yourself to give thanks every day will eventually make it a routine. Soon, you will no longer live without gratitude, as you will want to experience the feeling that thanksgiving brings each day. Start by writing them down; feel them as you write. Over time, you will notice even more reasons for gratitude emerging. You will begin to recognize the good things already present in your life. But recognizing them requires focus and attention. Practice optimism by finding the good in every situation, as both positive and negative aspects exist in life. You will experience more of what you focus on and give energy to. Not a single day goes by without me expressing gratitude, and I can confidently say it has transformed my life. I wake up and say, "Thank you." I look at myself in the mirror and say it again: "Thank you." Even when something unpleasant happens, I express gratitude for the lesson learned and the opportunity to grow.

When I give, I give thanks for the opportunity to give. I thank the other person who made it possible for me to experience this joy. When you do something for another, there is no other person—it is you, and only you. The other is you, and you are the other. Everything is connected to everything that exists. What you do for others, you do for yourself. What you do for yourself, you do for others. By giving thanks and giving, everything grows in your life because you demonstrate that you have abundance. Gratitude should not just be a mantra; it should be felt within. What we give thanks for and feel in our hearts is what we will create. Be grateful for both the good and the bad, for this is accepting life's duality—understanding that every pain or problem carries a gift within itself. Consciously return to what you have in the present moment. In the most difficult moments of my life, when I thought my life had no meaning, I realized the true power of gratitude. At that time, I did not know that one day I would be thankful for what had happened to me, for it shaped the way I live today. The oaks that endure the strongest winds grow deeper roots, becoming more powerful and resilient in the face of storms. Today, I am thankful for all the challenges and hardships in my life. They have made me stronger, and they have shaped me into who I am now.

"The strongest blows of the opponent have always made me stronger."

Muhammad Ali

In those moments, I learned how powerful our bodies are and that they have the ability to heal themselves. Not only that, but I also felt the power of gratitude for the gifts I received effortlessly. Gratitude brought me back to my true self, and I can confidently say that if you consciously accept everything that has happened to you and give thanks, your life will take on a new dimension—one of gratitude and strength. Through my body's illness, I found endless gratitude because it made me realize the true value of my health. Without experiencing sickness, we cannot fully appreciate health. Without knowing poverty, we cannot truly understand the value of wealth. And without enduring suffering, we cannot comprehend the depth of happiness. In my visualization, I saw myself happy, full of life, dancing, and smiling. I gave thanks from the bottom of my heart for that vision, and today, I am living it. Not only do I now experience the things I was once grateful for, but I also receive even more blessings—things I could never have imagined. Life is full of gifts, and it's up to you whether you choose to shift your energy and embrace them with gratitude or remain ungrateful and fail to see the good things you already have. When you cultivate this level of awareness, your life will be filled with joy, fulfillment, and abundance.

Be thankful, even for something you don't yet have, for the feeling of gratitude brings fulfillment and allows it to become part of your reality. Feel it. Send out the frequencies necessary to manifest what you desire in your life. To give thanks before seeing it is to believe. The energy of gratitude is powerful—it acts like a magnet. Over time, your body's energy will feel abundant because gratitude transforms your state of being, allowing you to live happily. After all, it is not the happy person who gives thanks, but the one who gives thanks who becomes happy. Gratitude is the energy that connects us with God.

Now, stop reading, take a deep breath, and say, **"Thank you for this gift!"**

CHAPTER

CHANGE YOUR HABITS, CHANGE YOUR LIFE!

Habits are stable behaviors that we engage in repeatedly over time. By nature, all people are fundamentally similar; it is their habits that distinguish them. As Confucius aptly stated, "Only their habits differ."

Our brain registers habits in order to conserve energy, making them automatic. Once a habit is formed, it no longer requires conscious attention, as maintaining focus consumes considerable energy. Nature has designed this mechanism to help preserve the body's resources. Habits also simplify life significantly. Without them, survival would be more challenging, as the body relies on established routines. For example, we brush our teeth, read, drive a car, and eat at specific times without consciously thinking about every individual action—all because these behaviors have become ingrained habits. However, habits can also contribute to health problems, hinder personal growth, and limit our potential—particularly when they stem from a lack of awareness or understanding.

WE ALL HAVE BAD HABITS

Many of us engage in detrimental behaviors, such as excessive phone use, overconsumption of alcohol, overeating, smoking, or watching movies that leave us feeling negative. These habits can prevent us from achieving our goals.

As **Albert Einstein once said**, "*The purest form of insanity is doing the same thing over and over again and expecting different results.*"

How to Change Habits?

It typically takes between 21 and 60 days to form or change a habit. Often, individuals seek advice from others and try to change multiple habits simultaneously. However, this approach is overwhelming for the body, which needs energy to register a new habit. Attempting to adopt too many changes at once often leads to frustration and a return to old habits. Instead, focus on adopting one new habit each month.

I will share the habits that have transformed my life and the lives of many others. You can also mark these habits on your calendar to track your progress and stay motivated.

January	
February	
March	
April	
May	
July	
August	
September	
October	
November	
December	

THE SIX BEST HABITS THAT WILL CHANGE YOUR LIFE

Sports

Engaging in sports strengthens your desire to take action, disciplines you, and enhances your social life. It boosts your confidence, and the brain releases endorphins, which contribute to feelings of happiness. After exercising, you automatically feel better and experience a sense of empowerment. Physical activity raises your energy levels, which in turn increases your productivity. Humans are inherently made to move and be active. While I do not recommend any specific sport, it is important to engage in an activity that brings you joy.

Morning Routine

The way you begin your day significantly influences how the rest of the day unfolds. Start your day with gratitude and a positive outlook, setting optimistic expectations. Meditate for 20 minutes, then take a few moments to plan and organize your day. Write down how you want to live, as this creates positive momentum, elevates your vibration, and attracts people who share the same energy.

Reading

Although we are taught many basic subjects in school, topics such as how to live happily or achieve financial freedom are often not part of the curriculum. Many people believe that once they finish school and earn a degree, their learning journey ends. However, reading is a valuable source of knowledge about life, health, finances, relationships, and happiness. When reading, it is important not only to absorb the information but also to apply the lessons. The habits I am sharing with you, for example, have profoundly impacted my life.

Face Your Fears

We all carry various fears, such as the fear of failure, rejection, or disapproval. These fears exist within our minds. The best way to overcome them is to confront them directly. Facing your fears requires courage and readiness. Courage does not mean the absence of fear; it means the ability to move forward despite it. For example, if you fear public speaking, practicing it is the most effective way to overcome that fear. Although not everyone may appreciate you, the more you practice, the easier it becomes. Visualize yourself doing what you fear, imagining everything going well. This mental rehearsal will help your body become accustomed to the situation, as it does not distinguish between real and imagined experiences. Over time, your fears will lessen, and you may find that the exact opposite of what you expect happens.

Socialize with Positive People!

As previously mentioned, the people we surround ourselves with influence both our beliefs and habits. If you spend time with positive and successful individuals, you will unconsciously adopt their ways of thinking, speaking, and living. On the other hand, spending time with individuals who gossip, complain, and maintain a negative outlook can trap you in a downward spiral. Socializing with people who radiate positivity will inspire you with good ideas and energies, helping you lead a more fulfilling life. They will motivate and support you, even in achieving your most ambitious goals.

Try New Things, Learn New Things!

Step outside your comfort zone and embrace new experiences! Learn, grow, and take action—move forward. We are designed to evolve and make changes in our lives. We are not here merely to read and meditate; we are here to live fully, regardless of the circumstances. Whether it's discovering a new passion, reading another book, taking a new course, or trying a new sport, each new experience contributes to your growth. Even something as simple as taking a walk in an unfamiliar place can make a difference. As you try new things, you will feel happier, more productive, and more motivated. This openness helps you find your passion. Trying new activities not only brings pleasure but also introduces you to new people, fresh perspectives, and exciting opportunities. Consequently, your life will take on a richer and more vibrant quality.

Chapter

6

Intuition

"Your time is limited, so don't waste it living someone else's life. Don't be trapped by dogma— which is living with the results of other people's thinking. Don't let the noise of others' opinions drown out your inner voice. And most importantly, dare to follow your heart and intuition. They somehow already know what you truly want to become."
Steve Jobs

A blind man gets lost on a mountain and suddenly falls, only to come across a man lying on the ground. As the blind man touches the spot where he fell with his stick, he realizes that the other man cannot walk. The two of them begin to talk, and both complain about their fate.

"Ever since I started thinking, I've been lost on this mountain and don't know how to get out because I can't see," says the blind man.

"I've been lying here since I started thinking, and I can't get off the mountain because I can't walk," replies the man who cannot move.

As they continue talking, trying to find a way out of their predicament, the immobile man has an idea and tells the blind man that if he carries him on his back, he can guide the way, and together they can escape the mountain.

In this story, the blind man symbolizes reason, while the immobile man represents intuition. We, too, will find our way off the mountain when we learn to use both.

Many people wonder what intuition is and how to connect with it. When we accept that there is a vast intelligence in the universe, the real question becomes how to align ourselves with it. This intelligence knows more than we do, and in the chaotic times we live in, it can help us take a positive turn and reconnect with the source within us. Intuition has different meanings for different people, but for me, it is a deep wisdom within-one that emerges when we stop questioning with the mind and start listening with the heart.

We use the mind to hear the heart. Often, we believe that the mind is meant to ask questions, while the heart is meant to provide answers—sending us signals about what to pursue and impulses to act in ways that serve our highest good. At times, I have feared the answers my intuition has given me because they did not lead to the easy path, but rather the difficult, yet right, one.We have been taught to listen to the opinions of others rather than our own intuition. This has distanced us from ourselves, causing us to live in disharmony for years. True fulfillment comes, however, when we reconnect with our inner wisdom and bring it into our reality. Feel it. Tune into the frequencies that align with what you want to manifest in your life. On my journey, I have learned how to access information and connect with the great wisdom that lies within us. In today's world, we have become accustomed to relying solely on the mind, which is inherently limited compared to intuition. The great universal power flows through intuition, yet we have set it aside in favor of our rational mind, which, by nature, has its constraints. The rational mind can only process information based on past life experiences. However, intuition—often referred to as the voice of God—is connected to the vast wisdom and knowledge of cosmic intelligence. It has the ability to provide us with the right information at the perfect moment. Life becomes easier and more beautiful when we learn to trust and listen to our intuition. Since I began following my inner voice, my life has transformed for the better.

How did I start receiving information, images, and feelings through intuition?

I envisioned myself standing before people, helping and advising them. In my dream, I saw myself healing others. One day, after months of meditation, I reached a beautiful state of peace—an indescribable feeling. Before entering meditation, I had asked myself a question: *Is this truly who I am? Is my mission to inspire and help others?* A part of me hesitated, as my mind was still questioning whether I knew enough or was adequately prepared for such a role. Yet, deep down, I knew I had already helped those around me by offering new perspectives and guiding them toward positive change. Doubt lingered, but something within me affirmed that this was my purpose on earth—and that I could succeed. My faith in my own power outweighed my uncertainty.

In my vision, I saw myself at an age somewhere between 55 and 60 years old. I can't say exactly, but I was at peace. For a few seconds, I felt as if I were truly living in that moment. Then, as I began questioning why I was seeing this image—who she was and why this vision had appeared-my mind became confused, and the picture vanished. I was surprised, as nothing like this had ever happened to me before, even though I had followed my intuition in many aspects of my life. Later, when I returned to my apartment, I watched a video about signs from the universe and how we receive guidance from an inexhaustible source of wisdom. That's when I realized that my vision had been a clear message from my intuition, urging me to continue this journey. In that moment, I understood that I had received the right answers to my questions. Since then, I have continued asking myself important questions-and I have received answers in various forms: through books, emotions, and even mental images.

I can tell you this-when you silence the external noise and start truly listening to your intuition, you will begin to receive guidance. At first, it may be scary because the path will not always be easy, but all the barriers will eventually fall away. You will become more confident and courageous.

For a long time, I was afraid to speak in public. Deep inside, I held a belief that I was not meant to speak much-simply because I was a woman. This belief had blocked me for years, causing me to withdraw and remain silent, despite knowing so much. But on my journey, I discovered that where fear exists, hidden potential also lies.

I want to tell you that when you start listening to your intuition, the path ahead may not always be easy. Your mind might resist, tangled in old programs and blockages, creating confusion. But trust that this is the right path-the one meant for you. It is safe because intuition never leads you astray; it always guides you toward your most authentic journey. Your intuition reveals the unique path designed for you, unfolding the gifts you were meant to bring into this life. When you follow it, you align with your true purpose, stepping into the life that was always waiting for you.

CHAPTER

MEDITATION

Lie down or sit comfortably. Relax and close your eyes. Take a slow, deep breath in, and gently release it. With each exhale, feel your body relaxing more and more. Calm your mind and let your thoughts flow—don't try to stop them. Imagine your mind becoming as still and peaceful as a serene lake. Shift your attention to the area of your solar plexus chakra. Imagine that within you lies a deep intelligence, and you can sense its presence. This wisdom is a part of you. You can communicate with it, ask questions, and receive guidance.

As you do this, relax your mind and allow the answers to come naturally. The responses may appear as images, words, or feelings. True answers are clear, pure, and rooted in the present—free from the past or future. You will recognize their truth. If no answer comes, do not force it. Instead, move through your day and let insights arise naturally. They may come through books, conversations, or unexpected moments of clarity.

Ask your intuition: *What should I learn from this? What should I do in this situation?* Trust the feeling that follows. If the answer comes from your intuition, you will feel alive and at peace. If it comes from fear or doubt, it is the voice of the ego, not intuition.

Trusting and listening to your intuition takes practice. The more you attune to it, the easier it becomes. You will begin to recognize the hidden power within you—always ready to guide and support you. As you grow more sensitive to this inner wisdom, your sense of what is best for you will become clearer.

Intuition is always available, whenever you need it. It opens up to you the moment you choose to trust your inner knowing.

CHAPTER

TRUST YOUR INTUITION!

We have been taught to trust others and follow their instructions. In doing so, we lose touch with our intuition-our inner voice, or the voice of the soul-whatever you choose to call it. This disconnection is one of the reasons why people often feel depressed, helpless, and empty. However, we can learn to reconnect with ourselves, to align with the inner truth that comes through intuition.

Human beings are often afraid of the unknown, even though it has always been present. The heart continually strives to bring us back to life, to trust the wisdom within us that knows what is best. This guiding force leads us through life. Trusting intuition means letting go of everything we've accumulated and simply surrendering to it. Sometimes, it may not show us the easy way, but rather the right way for us.

Our minds can become very confused, and when intuition provides us with guidance or an impulse, we may mentally block it by thinking, "What if it doesn't happen? What if I can't do it? What if I'm not ready?" We want to protect ourselves, but as you've heard, the heart gives impulses to the mind—so listen to the heart. But today, how many people truly listen to their inner voice? How many live according to what their soul desires? Many people know deep down what they want, but their minds become clouded. These confusions stem from the programs we internalize by constantly listening to external influences.

Learn to ask your inner self questions, and you will receive answers.

WHAT EXACTLY DOES IT MEAN TO TRUST INTUITION?

It means that, in every situation, at every moment, we should trust the feelings within us-the voice of the soul-and act from there. This guidance can help us live lives we love and fulfill our desires. Sometimes, you might have doubts about trusting something that feels illogical, as your feelings may sometimes tell you not to do something, and you may hesitate to avoid hurting others. However, others will also benefit from your being true to yourself and listening to your inner voice.

Your changes-and when you say no on different occasions-might irritate others because they are used to you adapting to them. But believe that your way of being in harmony with yourself will help others too. You don't have to overthink things; some people will love you just as you are, and some may leave. That's okay. Everyone needs time to grow, and if someone has a deeper connection with you, you will meet again. A new life will begin for you when you start to trust your inner voice.

Be willing to make mistakes, because if you make a mistake once, you'll do better the next time. Learning to trust your inner voice is an art. Like any art, it takes time and practice to master it. Intuition is always correct, but it takes time to understand it.

I know it is not easy to hear the voice of intuition and distinguish it from the other voices inside us. The voices of different programs we carry often make us question what the true voice of intuition is. For example, if you want something for yourself and your inner voice tells you to call a certain person, but you don't do it because your mind gets confused for many reasons, know that you didn't act correctly. That person might have shown you something important that could have helped you achieve exactly what you wanted.

Another example: your inner voice tells you that you feel tired and want to rest, but your mind tells you that you must keep going. If you ignore the feeling of fatigue, by the end of the day, you may feel drained, anxious, and unable to focus. If you had listened to your intuition and taken a moment to pause and rest, you would have felt clearer, more relaxed, and accomplished all that you had set out to do-still full of energy at the end of the day.

This happens to many people every day because they are simply "doing" without listening to their bodies. Even when the body asks for rest, the mind keeps pushing, creating a contradiction between the body and the mind.

Become an observer of yourself.

Pay attention to how you feel when you follow the guidance of your mind versus your intuition. Over time, you'll prove that what comes from intuition feels easy, powerful, and in flow. When you suppress these feelings and ignore your intuition, you will feel drained and experience emotional and physical pain. Don't be hard on yourself if these things happen-learning takes time. Old habits are deeply ingrained, and it takes time to unlearn them.

By practicing daily, you will reconnect with your power and learn to listen to your inner voice. Make it a habit to go within each day, meditate, and ask for help. Ask questions, and you'll receive answers in various forms: through books, videos, feelings, or a conversation with a friend. Your body helps guide you, and this is how you begin making decisions from within, from the intelligence inside you—not from your head. Decisions will become easier.

You don't have to overthink things, even though I've written extensively about intuition. It's a natural process; we've just been taught not to listen to it. Energy will flow naturally through your body. This is also the moment when many things will shift, and you may lose some friendships or people in your life. They will leave you, but you won't care as much, because once you are aligned with your energy, you won't feel the need to do things you don't enjoy. You will work with your body, listen to your intuition, and it will feel like you've entered a new phase of life. You will experience power and freedom.

For example, if your inner voice tells you to call someone but you hesitate due to confusion or fear, know that you didn't act correctly. That person may have offered valuable insight that could have helped you achieve what you desired.

Chapter

Change Your Reality by Changing Your Beliefs

Reality exists as we see it!
Whatever you believe, you have in your life!
The story of the sleeping lion

A pregnant lioness sees a herd of sheep and says, "Oh my goodness, I've got lunch!" While she tries to catch a sheep, the hunter captures and kills the lioness. With her last strength, she manages to give birth to the cub, but she does not survive her wounds and dies. The hunter takes pity on the cub, takes it, and raises it with the sheep. The lion grows up like a sheep and does everything the sheep do. Since the sheep know that the lion is not a sheep, they treat him with respect. However, the lion feels unloved and unaccepted. A few days later, another lion comes and thinks the same thing as the lioness: "Oh, I've got my lunch!" The lion tries to attack a sheep. However, as he attempts to bite the sheep, he sees the little lion. He asks the little lion what he is doing there.

The little lion is very afraid. He begs the lion not to harm him. "Please, lion, I'm just a little sheep. Don't eat me!" And the lion says to the little lion, "Open your eyes, because you are a lion — you are not a sheep. Why are you acting like this? You are the king of animals. Act like a lion!" The little lion did not understand what the big lion wanted from him. He didn't understand at all. The little lion was so convinced that he was a sheep.

The big lion takes the little lion and sends him to a river. He puts his head in the water to wake up his reflexes. He says, "Look, you are not a sheep — you are a lion." Once again, he puts his head in the water, and then the little lion realizes that he was not a sheep but a lion. From there, he begins to believe that he has greater strength than he thought — he has the strength of a lion, the strength that nature had given him. None of us is born helpless. Without self-confidence and self-esteem, we are like an empty notebook, and we allow ourselves to take on the beliefs of others, beliefs which have not done us any good. We are alienated by the beliefs of others, and we think that we are someone else, not who we truly are. We, too, like the little lion, are blind, thinking we are what we believe about ourselves. But this can be changed by changing the way we think and feel — that is, by changing our beliefs. Now, one might ask why we have thoughts, and the answer is: to create. But most thoughts come from our subconscious. It is where beliefs are programmed — an image of who we think we are.

"Thoughts and emotions are deeply interconnected, and both are shaped by life experiences. Of course, thoughts are also influenced by emotions, and they, in turn, shape our reality. Research indicates that only 5% of what we create is done consciously. The most effective way to become aware of the programs within ourselves and begin to transform them is through the trance state, which is achieved through meditation. Our brain functions as a supercomputer, capable of processing an infinite amount of data. Everything we have internalized over the years is recorded and subsequently presented to us externally in a manner consistent with our perceptions. Even the laws of nature manifest in this way, suggesting that everything external is a reflection of our beliefs-of our thoughts and emotions. I have found it challenging to fully grasp Albert Einstein's statement: 'There is no such thing as reality, but only the reality that we observe.' This means that as we think and believe we are, we will become. What we believe about life will be demonstrated to us. For instance, if we believe that others lie, deceive, or that the world is a dangerous place, we will encounter a reality that reflects these beliefs."

The world can often be perceived as a dangerous place, filled with suffering and disappointment, leading us to form limiting beliefs. These beliefs, such as "No one is happy" or "Life is inherently painful," are often shaped by personal experiences. For instance, if Ana, after a painful divorce, comes to believe that all men are untrustworthy or flawed, she may start encountering individuals who reinforce this negative view. As a result, Ana might close herself off from the possibility of love, assuming that all men are the same, based on her past experience. This perception becomes Ana's reality, as her belief system attracts circumstances that align with her expectations. However, if Ana were to become aware that her soul's journey involves navigating the dualities of life—where experiencing what love is not helps her recognize true love—she might shift her perspective. By changing her beliefs and raising her vibration, she could create space for a new kind of relationship, one that resonates with her transformed energy. Ultimately, the key to attracting different experiences lies in her ability to understand that the opposite of her previous relationship exists within her potential, and that transformation starts from within.

To whom Ana has created its opposite during the contrasts with the first person, and only needs to change her belief, raise her vibration, and the person who will be in resonance with her will come into her life. But she must first receive a new thought, feel it, and believe that the opposite of what she thought exists.

THIS ALSO APPLIES TO HEALTH

If we have negative thoughts, we read about diseases, and now we don't think much about it, but our consciousness registers everything we consume every day. With this, we begin to think that something is wrong with us, that if someone is sick, it must be us, or why not us. We start reading about that disease and feed the thought with negative energy, from which the first symptoms and perhaps the disease itself begin to develop. I don't want to scare you with this, but as we think, so our health will be. As we think about our partners, so they will be. As we think about finances, so they are. The outside world is a mirror of our beliefs.

How are beliefs formed?

Imagine a belief like a four-legged table. In other words, the table is the thought, then the mind seeks confirmation, receives perhaps three or four experiences, and a stable table is created—that is, a belief. Throughout our lives, we have changed our beliefs a lot. For example, we loved a song and then heard it over and over until it became one of our favorites, or we tried a certain food and kept enjoying it until it became part of our routine. Our beliefs, like this, are shaped by repeated thoughts, experiences, and perceptions. However, beliefs can also limit us if we don't consciously evaluate them. For instance, if we repeatedly think about something negative, like poor health, we might subconsciously align with those thoughts, attracting more of the same energy. To change this, we must consciously shift our beliefs by replacing old thoughts with new ones that resonate with the positive reality we desire. When it comes to health, relationships, or finances, what we think and feel becomes our reality. The power lies in shifting our mindset, raising our vibration, and consciously embracing the belief that a positive shift is possible. As we change the internal narrative, the external world will begin to mirror it, bringing in healthier, more abundant experiences. It's all interconnected—what we believe shapes what we experience.

We can change our beliefs;

We just have to be willing and ready. How to change our beliefs? To change a belief, we must first break the four legs of the table, meaning we need to change the experiences we have. Start by searching for a thought you want to change. Then, find at least three experiences that support that thought. Finally, transform the negative thought into a positive one.

Examples

The world is a dangerous place" – "In the world I live in, everything is fine." "People are deceivers" – "Every day, I meet trustworthy people." "Money destroys character" – "Money gives me the opportunity to do what I want." "No one is completely healthy" – "Health is our true nature." There are many other thoughts you can choose and seek experiences or people who embody love, health, and financial abundance. Then, adopt the beliefs of these people. I have acquired books, knowledge, and lessons from people who live this way, and I've allowed new thoughts to bring new emotions. Over time, my reality has changed. Now, you live in the reality where you are because you have different beliefs about life that you've accepted and recorded in your consciousness, and you live them every day, every moment. The good news is that you can change your reality. The challenge is that we are trained to notice reality rather than consciously create it. We see one thing, and reality reflects that back to us, making us believe that this is the way it is and that we can't do anything about it. Now, read this book because you are on a journey of rising awareness. It has also been established by some scientists that our thoughts and emotions have a direct impact on our cells. Our thoughts, therefore, affect our health. We make our bodies sick with negative thoughts, which block us from achieving good health and creating what we want. We are held back from being successful because of negative thoughts and beliefs, and, as mentioned earlier, we are programmed to think that we cannot succeed. In fact, we tend to become what we think and believe about ourselves. Our lives are a reflection of our beliefs! You can change your beliefs and, consequently, your reality! We often identify with our thoughts. In meditation, you become an observer of your thoughts and realize that you are not your thoughts. Over time, by becoming aware of what you think, where those thoughts come from, and who influenced them, you can change those beliefs. Associate with people who have a different outlook on life. They don't have to be physically with you. Today, you can learn from people who live completely differently from you. I know that in the beginning, you might defend your beliefs because you will perceive them as true—because you create them through your thoughts and feelings. But be open to new lessons and new thoughts that will bring you happiness, peace, good health, and financial success.

Most people are afraid to even think that they can live like this. Believe that you can be healthy, happy, and have everything you need in life. I am a person who has moved into a completely different reality from the one I had before. My book, "Believe in Your Power," provides the methods to help you change what you don't like. In the work I do, I see people transforming their lives every day by embracing new thoughts about themselves, their past, their partners, life problems, finances, health, and more. For those who are tired of the life they lead and are ready to create what they want to live, it takes just one decision and the willingness to take responsibility. From that moment, their life begins to change and breathe differently.

One day, a farmer found an eagle egg and placed it among the chicken eggs. Along with the hatching of the chicken eggs, the eagle egg also hatched. The eagle grew up with the chickens as if they were its siblings and as if the chicken were its mother. Because it had grown up with the chickens, the eagle behaved just like them. It moved its wings and flew only as high as the chickens could. It dug in the ground with its feet to look for and eat insects, just like the chickens. Years passed, and the eagle grew old. One day, it looked up into the sky and saw a large bird that had spread its wings and was flying freely. Admiringly, the old eagle gazed at it in the sky. "Who is he?" the old eagle asked a chicken that was close by. "It's an eagle, the king of birds," answered the chicken. "Wouldn't it be wonderful if we, too, could fly in the sky like that?" asked the eagle. "Forget it-we are chickens," replied the chicken. The eagle forgot and went on with his life, dying with the belief that he was a chicken.

(African story)

Chapter

10

Emotional Pains

Many of us did not receive enough attention and love as children. But it is not only love and lack of attention that affect our lives-it is also all the other emotions we have experienced. This is the reason for many problems in adulthood, as people carry that lack with them for years without realizing that unlived or repressed emotions sometimes manifest as blockages that create diseases in our bodies. People carry emotional pain for years without knowing where it comes from. It is fascinating how, in therapy, people can release emotions within minutes-emotions they may have carried in their bodies for 10, 20, 30, or even more years. Most people are afraid to acknowledge and face emotions such as boredom, fear, anger, etc. They are afraid to feel and confront them because they think these emotions will consume them, but the opposite is true. The moment people open up and allow themselves to fully experience these emotions, they are released and cleansed from the body. When people let go of these emotions, they gain more life energy, heal, and live an easier life. If we carry bad feelings with us for years, they keep us in low energy and block us from creating the life we want. We must learn to be in touch with our emotions—live them, allow them, and change them if we wish. Some people come to me wanting to think positively and live a better life, but they are afraid to confront all the negative emotions stored in their bodies. Some have even fallen ill from hearing negativity from others.

Think positive, change your life! We live in a world where only when we accept everything within us can we truly love and accept ourselves. I'm not saying that we shouldn't change, but if we oppose change, we oppose nature-because everything in nature changes. With every emotion and every experience, we change too. To bring about quick change in the direction we desire, we must consciously begin creating by looking inward, confronting negativity, and addressing the low-vibration emotions within us. We must fully experience them as they were meant to be lived and then make peace with them. I have come to understand that pain is nothing more than the opposition of emotions. Take childbirth as an example-many women fear it, and their contractions work against the pain. The more they tighten their muscles, the more pain they experience. In the same way, we experience pain when we are afraid to feel an emotion. For the body, pain serves as a defense mechanism, protecting it from danger. But emotionally, too, when we resist our emotions, we experience pain. All feelings are a part of life, creating a rainbow in which we live. I will explain two low-vibrational emotions so you can understand them and release them!

Anger

With some people I've worked with, after they started to regain their strength, they sometimes began to feel anger and would come to me, asking why they were experiencing these emotions. They wondered why they were raising their voices and reacting in ways they never had before. I explained to them that people in depression often feel nothing but emptiness and suppressed anger. As they slowly begin to regain their strength, these emotions start to surface. Yes, anger is a low-vibration emotion, but it is slightly higher than depression. Allow yourself to feel the anger, and imagine a volcano erupting inside you, filling you with energy and power. If you don't fully experience this emotion, you will attract people into your life who repeatedly trigger it-a message that unprocessed anger still exists within you. If you feel anger, express it in a safe space where you are alone. Let it out—scream if you need to. You can also work with a therapist, hitting a pillow or finding another way to release it without causing harm. People who have given away their power to others often feel angry because they are not in control of their own strength. When you learn to take your life into your own hands and confront the pain within you, you will fully experience and release that blockage. Often, we create anger as a defense mechanism to protect ourselves from deeper wounds. When you step into your strength, you create your life as you desire, not as others expect. When creative energy flows through you, and you fully accept all the emotions within, your energy will naturally move through your body, transforming your entire state of being. We often need support to release emotional blockages. Seek a therapist who can help you work through them, as guidance can be essential in this process. Find someone you resonate with—someone you trust to explore your emotional world together. If you want to help yourself, which you absolutely can, take a moment during the day to check in with yourself. Ask: How do I feel? What is this feeling trying to tell me? Why am I having this thought? Allow yourself to fully experience the emotion, feel it, and then let it go.

Fear

Everything we run away from follows us-especially fear. The fears we experienced as children still exist within us. Often, when working with the inner child, people ask where that child is. The answer is simple: every fear you faced as a child but never confronted still lives within you. Your inner child still cries out in fear. Now, as an adult, you may fear losing your partner. Jealousy, for example, is not just about the fear of losing someone-it often runs deeper. In my work as a therapist, I've encountered many cases where people's fears are not about specific situations but about the fear of being left alone. As a child, you may have been alone, felt abandoned, or lost a parent due to separation or illness. That fear still lingers, but now it manifests in different ways-jealousy, fear of flying, fear of heights, and more. It is fascinating how everything is recorded in our brain and nervous system. The moment we first experience fear, if we soothe our inner child, the emotion subsides. The inner child is not a separate entity but rather the emotion we felt at that moment-it was imprinted in our system, and our body remembers everything. When we enter a trance state, we uncover the root cause of our present-day panic, fears, or emotional blockages. Many fears have been imprinted in our bodies since childhood, subtly influencing us every day. However, when I speak of fear here, I am not referring to the natural fear that serves as a protective mechanism for the body. That type of fear is part of our survival instinct-our body's automatic response to danger, activating the "fight or flight" system. For example, if we encounter a dangerous situation while driving, our body instinctively reacts to protect us. This is a natural and necessary response. However, we often continue to scare ourselves by consuming fearful content-watching frightening images, reading disturbing news—and in doing so, we create an imbalance in the body. Our nervous system is not designed to process excessive amounts of fear. When the brain continuously releases stress hormones, it disrupts our well-being, as anything in excess can be harmful to us. Fear, derived from the Latin angustus, signifies constriction. It generates emotions such as anger and helplessness. Where fear exists, love cannot flourish. Therefore, to open the gateway to love in life, one must confront all fears. It is possible to transform fear into a source of growth and even pleasure. Fear should not be perceived as an adversary; rather, it serves as a guide toward trust. Without an understanding of fear, one cannot fully comprehend love and trust. When fear is repressed rather than fully experienced, it gives rise to panic. Many individuals seek to avoid fear, yet in doing so, they inadvertently create further fear from the unresolved emotions within. This internal conflict leads to psychological blockages, manifesting as panic. Fear is an emotion I have encountered frequently. However, through achieving a state of calmness and directly confronting my fears, I have recognized that fear is intrinsically linked to other emotional states such as shame, guilt, anger, and helplessness. By engaging in inner healing, one can address these fears and nurture the inner child. To facilitate this process, I will provide a guided meditation. Engage with the text, practice meditation, and embark on the journey of inner healing.

CHAPTER

OVERCOMING EMOTIONAL DEPENDENCIES: EMBRACING FREEDOM AS A FUNDAMENTAL RIGHT

FREEDOM IS YOUR BIRTHRIGHT!

At this moment, I find myself in nature, which seems to be accompanying me-it speaks to me and dictates my words. I know, at times, I feel as if I am in a fairy tale, but if you truly understood, life is both a film and a fairy tale in which we are the actors. These roles we play are simply the ones we have chosen to experience in this lifetime. We are the directors of our own film, and we have consciously selected the roles we play long before the film itself began. I feel as though a great creative force is guiding me, compelling me to write these words. I may not always articulate what I see as beautifully as I experience it, but one thing is certain-happiness in life is directly connected to freedom. Only when we recognize that, in nature, nothing belongs to anything else, that everything is interconnected and exists in harmony, can we truly embrace this freedom. From the moment we begin to learn about life, we are influenced by those around us. However, the majority of them have never learned how to live freely, as they themselves have never been free. Even though a person reaches adulthood, typically around 18 to 20 years of age, and is considered ready to live independently, they still carry years of emotional dependency. The expectations and emotional deficiencies we inherit hinder our ability to fully embrace a life of true freedom and autonomy.

Meditate on this idea-turn inward and feel whether you are truly free! The path to freedom lies in inner awareness. Many people unconsciously carry emotional dependencies rooted in their personal deficiencies. To fill these voids, they often turn to external sources such as relationships, substances like alcohol and drugs, or habits like smoking, believing these will compensate for what they lack internally. However, true happiness is not found in emotional dependency. We must free ourselves from all emotional attachments and recognize that fulfillment comes from within, rather than relying on others to provide what we feel is missing. Often, we expect people to behave in ways that align with our desires. We seek validation, love, and happiness through them, making our emotions contingent on their actions. However, such expectations lead to disappointment, as they stem from emotional dependence. If we wish to be free, we must also allow others to be free—this is the foundation of unconditional love. Love cannot be tied to expectations because true love, in its purest form, is divine. It exists without conditions or demands. Emotional freedom means giving without expecting anything in return, as everything flows naturally. When we release our dependencies on others, we experience a state of self-sufficiency, where our happiness is not dictated by external factors. Freedom does not mean detachment from love, but rather loving in a way that respects the autonomy of others. Your freedom ends where another person's begins. Thus, allow others to be free so that you too may fully experience your own freedom. I will not speak of guilt, as nothing truly belongs to anyone, and no one owes anything to anyone. To understand freedom, one must first comprehend that fulfillment cannot be attained through possession or control over another person. When you release others from expectations, you free yourself as well. Emotional dependence is particularly evident in close relationships, such as those between parents and children, friendships, and romantic partnerships. Here, dependence often disguises itself as love. Key Signs of Emotional Dependence Feeling that You Love Your Partner More Than Yourself If you abandon your personal interests, passions, friendships, and desires to conform to your partner's needs—prioritizing their happiness over your own—it is a sign of emotional dependence. You cannot be happy with someone else if you are not happy with yourself. True fulfillment cannot be found in a place where your own joy is absent.

When you go somewhere and you can't be happy without your partner, and you can't enjoy the place you're in because you miss them:

- **Nothing makes sense if your partner is not there with you.**
- **You are very jealous and want to constantly control your partner.**

The thought of being without them may cause anxiety, leading you to believe that your life would lose meaning without their presence. However, emotional dependence ultimately diminishes your sense of self, as you lose sight of what is truly beneficial for you. In many cases, emotional dependence leads to the breakdown of relationships. This often happens because an overly dependent person does not give their partner the space to grow. It is similar to gripping a glass too tightly-eventually, it shatters under pressure. Likewise, excessive attachment can damage the relationship rather than strengthen it. When a breakup occurs, the emotionally dependent person often feels completely lost, as if their life no longer has meaning. This is because they have placed their entire existence in someone else's hands. However, it is not the partner who has destroyed them-it is the dependency they built around that person that has caused their suffering. In most cases, individuals with emotional dependence attract partners who are similarly dependent. Within the challenges of their relationship, they mirror each other's emotional wounds, highlighting the unresolved fears and attachments they both carry. These struggles provide an opportunity for growth-if both partners are willing to process their emotional dependencies, they can move closer to true self-love and emotional liberation. Within each of us exists an abundance of love. However, in order to access it, we must first recognize and overcome the emotional barriers we have accumulated along our journey-those very obstacles that have distanced us from our true selves.

Your task is not to seek love, but to understand yourself and address the emotional barriers you have built against love.

I will offer several points that may help you free yourself from emotional dependencies. There are many pieces of advice on how to liberate yourself from emotional dependence, and some of these relate to learning how to love and value yourself. Below are a few additional suggestions:

The first step is to become aware that you are emotionally dependent on another person. Many people confuse this with love, but it has little to do with love itself; rather, it is about fulfilling your own emotional deficiencies through another person. In fact, individuals often use the other person to complete themselves, but it is important to be honest with yourself and assess whether you are emotionally attached. Identify the root cause, because this often stems from experiences in childhood, where you either had a relationship that lacked emotional fulfillment or failed to take responsibility for your own life. Consequently, you may have come to believe that you cannot live without the guidance of someone else or the presence of another individual.

Examine your beliefs and behaviors, as well as how you perceive yourself. Reflect on the relationships you have had, or the dynamic with your parents, mother, or siblings. Cultivating self-worth is crucial. Many of us were raised in a way that conditioned us to believe we had to achieve something in order to be valued, to listen to our parents, and only then were we recognized. However, they did not teach us that our inherent value is independent of these external factors. Focus on building your self-esteem. Consider what beliefs you hold about yourself. Work on enhancing your self-confidence by concentrating on the small daily successes you achieve and taking pride in the positive actions you undertake. Write down all the successes you've had and any compliments you've received. Engaging in this writing practice every day will train your brain to recognize the good, and over time, this will foster more positive experiences and increase your self-confidence.

Here are two exercises that may help you develop greater self-esteem:

1. Write down 5 to 10 successes you have achieved in your life. If you feel as though you have accomplished nothing or are unworthy, you have likely filled the gap within yourself with self-doubt. To fill this void with confidence and to value yourself, write down all the successes, no matter how small or seemingly insignificant, that you have experienced throughout your life.
2. Write down the things you do well. Document the actions you perform effortlessly, such as "I am precise, I am productive, I am accurate," etc.

A New Beginning

While traveling with my family to hike on Mount Pilatus here in Switzerland, I had an epiphany during the drive, where we typically listen to music. It became clear to me that the answers lie within us. I asked myself what connects two people and why one might use another to fulfill their own needs, or why someone forms an emotional bond with another. I experienced this with someone. After a few minutes of contemplation, while simply observing the road ahead, I received an answer. We come into this world with the purpose of gaining the experiences our soul needs, and we consciously accept forgetting who we are in order to remember during our lifetime.

When we are unaware of who we are, when we lose touch with our true selves, we spend our lives searching for it. Throughout this journey, everyone we encounter, with their experiences, serves to guide us toward rediscovering who we truly are. Thus, when we meet another person, at first, love develops as an initial commitment to discovering who we are. However, after several years, the process of polarity occurs, the opposite begins to manifest. The partner often overlooks the darker aspects that we must work through on our own. In this sense, they help us confront and purify those parts of ourselves. By doing so, we gain insight into these aspects, enabling us to integrate and learn from the experiences we have had.

CHAPTER

THE INNER CHILD

When I speak about the inner child, I am referring to all the experiences we, as children, have lived through. All the emotional wounds, fears, worries, accusations, and coldness in family relationships. The goal of therapy or meditation, the work with the inner child, is to establish a connection between your present self and the wounded child within you. This means working with your inner self to reconnect with the source of joy, happiness, and intuition. Working with the inner child means healing the pain within us, which still resides in our bodies. It is about accepting those wounds with love and not letting them guide our lives. We should not unconsciously create from those wounds, because, although we are adults now, we can still react with anger and negative emotions without knowing where they come from. Our subconscious mind is the place where all experiences are gathered, everything we have absorbed through our five senses. Through healing the inner child, we become aware that it is not us who feel jealousy now, but rather the fear within us as children, which we still carry with us unconsciously. So, we may react with anger because the inner child remembers how others treated us with anger, and we have carried that emotion with us. And this applies to all emotions we have gathered throughout our lives.

MEDITATION

Heal the Inner Child!

Sit down and keep your back straight. You can let your hands rest by your sides. Imagine that your breathing is like a gentle wave from the natural flow of life. With each breath, this gentle wave completely relaxes your body. Take a few deep breaths and pay attention to where this wave of breath stops in your body-there, you may find resistance. Allow the flow of your breath to release that blockage. Breathe deeply, and when you exhale, let go of all the muscles in your body, making sure your feet feel completely relaxed and heavy. Take a breath, allowing your stomach to release and feel warm and heavy. Now, feel your chest, arms, head, and the entire musculature of your face. Finally, your eyes should feel relaxed and heavy.

Now, recall a pain you have experienced, whether as a child or as an adult. Remember a situation where you were hurt or upset. Allow yourself to connect with that pain. Let this feeling arise. Now, feel it completely, because you have already experienced this feeling before. You even remember the place and time when you felt it, perhaps in a room, outside, or at school. See yourself in that place, struggling with that feeling. Perhaps your parents treated you harshly, or maybe you were punished. Or someone else hurt you.

Now, imagine that you are going to that room or place where you were and see yourself as a little child. You see yourself, wounded, perhaps in tears, and you tell yourself your name. Look at how the child looks you in the eyes. Tell them that you are here now, that they are not alone, that you love and respect them. Tell them that they are safe, protected, and everything will be okay. Let them know that they are no longer alone.

Now, be the loving adult that the child needed back then. Embrace them and let them be close to you. Gently touch their back and assure them that they are no longer alone. Tell them that you will always be there for their fears, pains, worries, and heartbreaks. Tell them that you are here to bring them joy and happiness.

Look the child in the eyes without judgment. Hug them with all your love. Feel the child inside of you, and feel all of their pain. Tell them that you will always be there for them. Now, the child feels better, they have received love, and they feel loved and protected.

After a few minutes, you can slowly open your eyes.

A New Beginning

This meditation helps you connect with all the wounds that still trouble you today, and perhaps you do not know where these pains come from, but they are waiting for you to heal them.

Practice this meditation several times. Learn the text, and you can adjust it as you wish or add important elements to it, so you can once again feel the pains that you can now release.

Some negative beliefs may originate from criticisms or judgments we encountered during childhood, and we might continue to carry them into adulthood. These include:

1. I may be perceived as selfish if I love myself.
2. I believe that others are responsible for my pain, and I feel powerless to heal it.
3. I am unworthy.
4. I cannot make myself happy, among others.

Through the process of working with the inner child, we can cultivate positive beliefs within ourselves, such as:

1. I am now mature enough to love myself, even though others may not have shown me love.
2. I embrace my emotions, including occasional upset, as I recognize that self-love has taught me that all emotions are a natural part of the human experience.
3. I am mature enough to care for myself and take responsibility for my own life.
4. I am open to new experiences and transformations in my life.
5. I am responsible for my own happiness.

CHAPTER

HOW TO LIVE IN BALANCE?

The lives of many people are becoming increasingly busy and stressed, constantly seeking more and more work, money, and wealth, until fatigue and collapse occur from the excessive hormones released by the brain during stress.

Due to the inability to achieve the goals and complete all that one demands from oneself, stress gradually starts to overwhelm the individual. The constant pressure of needing to do this and that work, to adapt to various people, to work hard, learn, and do what others are doing, creates stress and blocks the natural flow of life. So, what does it truly mean to flow with the stream of life? It means going where it is easiest, not forcing yourself, not suppressing yourself, not fighting against yourself, but rather listening to your emotions and following them.

Excessive stress has a negative impact on the body and on the expansion of our consciousness. The brain waves go completely out of control. As a result, we lose connection with our higher self or spirit, and we are no longer guided by our inner wisdom, but by external influences. We become hypnotized by external pressures, absorbing what others offer and give us. With excessive stress, problems arise with the neurons in the brain, leading to various physical ailments. Today's way of life often gives us the feeling that we are either running away from something or fighting. In this state, we are blocked from experiencing harmony, inner peace, and meaningful inner reflection.

However, for all those who feel stressed and suffer from ailments, are in anger or fear, I have good news-because this book is not in your hands by accident. You can change the brain waves and reconnect with the source within you, feel complete peace, and live in balance.

Everything we do in life should be done in a way that preserves balance. For example, when we work, we must know when to stop, take breaks, because no one is truly productive when constantly on the move. Today, people can hardly imagine themselves doing nothing. They are always in thought, planning, and demanding more from themselves, often more than they can give. Being in constant stress prevents the two hemispheres of the brain from communicating effectively, causing imbalance in the body, which leads to losing contact with oneself and with the source. If you have read about successful people, you know that the best ideas didn't come to them while they were working or thinking. They came when they were taking a shower, resting, or in a relaxed state, listening to themselves in a high energy state. To harmonize and heal yourself, to restore balance to your body, and to be as vital and happy as a child while connecting with the source within you, you must change the energy of your body. You need to learn to embrace rest and peace, and practice meditation. In meditation, the brain emits Theta waves at 4-8Hz, which gradually stabilize the body and take it deeper into a trance state. In this state, the immune system is strengthened, the body is cleansed, regenerated, and healed. Of course, this also requires inner work, education, and learning from those who live the life you aspire to live.

CHAPTER

PLAY AND WORK!

FIND YOUR PASSION!

Passion is the love of your being expressed through action.

It's crucial to understand that everything you do-if it's not done out of your own joy, out of passion, but because you feel it must be done-then you are not flowing with the river of life. The work you do should bring you pleasure, especially when you do it and don't even notice that time is flying by. When you follow your energy, then play and work become the same thing. Just like when you were a child, or even now, those things you desire to do, you do them with ease. It becomes a game for you, and there is no inner resistance; you can spend hours playing without realizing it. If you work, and you do what you love, you will be much more productive because you'll work far more than in a job you don't enjoy. The more joy you find in your work, the more you will be rewarded for it. It took me some time to find my passion, to discover what I could do to be in the flow of energy. There are three methods I've used, which you can also use to find your purpose or what makes you feel energized and do it with ease. Start by drawing a long vertical line and writing your birth date at the bottom. Then, write the years in order. In each year, as you start to learn about yourself, write down what you did with joy. Keep writing this until you reach the present year, and when you gather everything, you'll see it will give you some meaning. It will reveal something that perhaps even today tells you what flows easily for you, something you could do without much thought and as if it were a game. For example, if you've written down that you were a singer and also wrote lyrics, it could be that you're not meant to be a singer, but to write songs. Find it, maybe that's it-or something similar—but don't wait! Life is meant to be lived, to be moved, to try new things, and to make changes. So, begin and do something, and if what you're doing doesn't fulfill you or make you happy, then try something else, and each of these steps will prepare you to find your passion.

Life is created to be lived and enjoyed. Life is a gift, and it should be treated with care and love. Don't wait until you know exactly what makes you happy or what your passion is-move, try, and by trying, you'll come closer to what suits you best.

How to Find Your Passion?

We often take up something suggested by others because they tell us it's a secure job or an easy one. However, there is no such thing as a hard job when it's done with passion. It flows naturally, almost like a game. I, too, was advised to pursue accounting because it's considered a nice job, especially since I speak many foreign languages. But even then, I didn't feel like I had found myself in that field. Sometimes, parents who haven't fulfilled their own dreams-whether due to various reasons or a lack of courage-want their children to achieve what they themselves couldn't. The work you do to please or fulfill the wishes of your parents is still not your passion; it belongs to them. Work done with passion is joy, while work without passion leads to depression; it's a form of violence.

Another method to find your passion is to reflect on death.

Contemplating death gives depth to life. It's not death that we fear, but the idea that we haven't truly lived. That's why when you do what you love, when you live your passion, you live each moment fully because you are truly yourself. Form a cross, and in the top part, write what you would want others to say about you when you're no longer here. Believe me, this was the most powerful exercise for me when I understood why I am here. This exercise truly pushes you to express what you would want to hear. In the top section, write what you want a family member to say about you in front of others on the day of your funeral.

In the second section, write what you want a friend to say. In the third section, write what you want a colleague or boss to say. In the fourth section, choose someone you care about-whether it's your children or someone else-and write what you want them to say.

1. **Person X was a beloved brother, always there for me when I needed him.**I will never forget the moments with him because this person taught me how to love myself and have the courage to do what I want.
2. My friend has been a person who has set an example for the world. He has also changed my life by accompanying and supporting me whenever I needed it. We have shared many laughs together, and the hours we spent together flew by unnoticed because we enjoyed every moment, laughing and making jokes. We talked about beautiful things and helped each other to see further in what we do.
3. Person X has been a great person in what he has done and has left something for the world that was different in the world during the time he lived.
4. Write as you wish and make the text as it suits you and for as long as you want.

Do the exercise here!

- **A person from the family**
- **A friend**
- **A work colleague**
- **Person X**

WHY DEAL WITH DEATH?

So, I want to ask you a question because this topic has prompted me to start doing the things I want in my life.

If you were to die tomorrow, would you have lived your life fulfilled and satisfied because you lived the life you wanted?

This is a question you should ask yourself. Because this question might help you start a new life with fewer worries and to enjoy the moments of life.

You can close your eyes and go within yourself and feel what your true self means. You will immediately get an answer whether you are living happily or not. Your time and mine are limited, and with these exercises and going within, they have helped me start living my passion, living the way I want to, as my heart tells me. By reflecting on death, that one day I won't be here, I have started to not take things for granted. I am thankful for every day that is given to me—for sight, hearing, nourishment, the sun, the river, the air, for everything-and I feel a deep peace within me.

Do not waste the day on things you don't want to do because you are losing life, you are losing the most precious gift you have. I want to write about my experience, how I found it, why I am here, what my passion is, and the work I do today as play, and I can't imagine not doing it because it flows so naturally from within me.

When I stopped every job because I wasn't feeling well, I realized that everything I had done, my mind and goal were only to win and not to enjoy the work I was doing. But still, I don't call it the wrong path because there isn't one. All the journeys lead us back to ourselves, so life is a journey to our true self.

I started the journey within myself and began asking many questions about life. I did the exercise with the vertical line and saw that I had served as a child, I had been there for others. Even in school, I defended and helped others, on the street, in my family, in society. But still, I didn't have clarity on what my passion was.

After many years of meditation and self-work, I decided it was better not to do anything than to do something without my desire, something that didn't bring me joy.

By working on myself, spending more time with myself, I simply started doing it without even knowing that I was doing it because it flowed naturally. I helped neighbors, a friend to get out of different life situations. And there, a great desire opened up for me to help even more. From within, I saw myself speaking in front of others, but my mind didn't let me until I gained confidence to speak and write a book. I can't describe the energy I felt when I began living my passion. The results from people, the messages I received from them, their gratitude, etc., inspired me to do even more.

You can answer these 7 questions to help you find your passion!

If we try to reason with the mind, we cannot find the answer. We need to feel the mind because it can process 40 to 50 things, while the subconscious, the intuition, as the source that truly knows why we are here and what we are best at, has 40 million times more capacity. When we try to understand something with the mind or use it to find something, we are only using a small part of our full capacity.

Answer the questions and provide answers from within, feel them!

1. ***What did you enjoy most as a child?***
   Close your eyes and remember your childhood, feel what gave you joy.
2. ***What gives you great joy today when you do it, and you don't think much, you just do it?***
   Maybe you don't know what it is because you've been taught to listen to everyone else, but not to yourself. Ask yourself what you would do, and maybe you wouldn't even need to ask for anything for that work because you do it with joy.
3. ***What could this passion I have in the future bring for me to be happy?***
4. ***What would your dream life look like?***
   Sometimes we lack the courage to dream, to imagine what our life would look like if we lived our dreams, because we have that inner critic telling us we can't do it. We say we don't have time, that it's not certain, etc. Imagine that it has been fulfilled and see how your life looks now that your dream has come true.
   Where would you live? Who would you be with? What would you do every day? Would you work?
5. ***What would you do if everything went well?***
   Why this question? Because if it's something different from what

you are used to doing every day, then come the questions: could you do it too? Do you know how to do it? Do you have the ability?
You need to know beforehand if you can do it. Look for a form of security!

6. ***What would you do if money no longer played a role?***
   What would you do if you didn't earn money but continued doing it anyway?
   Many think that if they did what they want, they wouldn't earn anything, but it's the opposite. Because often, when people start doing what they love, opportunities arise for them to earn money doing it. We are in our creative energy, feeling fulfilled with energy because we love what we do.
7. ***How would you feel if you lived your dream, if you lived what fulfills you, what you feel from the depths of your being?***

Feel it, imagine it!

Maybe you won't get an answer immediately, but let the answer come from within. You may be overwhelmed with a lot of information or things you need to do. You've lost touch with yourself, with your intuition, but work with writing, write, ask these questions, and over time, you will get the right answer.

When you get the answer, grow, educate yourself, learn in that direction, keep it simple, start doing it, and along the way, you will learn, grow more and more, get ideas, connect with different people who will support you in fulfilling what you want in life.

Trust your intuition, live your dream, live your calling, your passion! When I asked myself these questions, I was dealing with death. I drew the vertical line, and over time, I just started living it. I started learning, meditating, listening to my inner self, listening to myself. I walked this journey, and it is mesmerizing to see how the paths open, how the ideas come, and how much support we have when we flow with the current of life. When we are in flow, we are in high energy.

HOW TO MAKE MONEY WITH PASSION?

If we think logically, we cannot understand how we could make money doing something we do with joy.

From the various beliefs we have about money, which I will write about in detail later, we think that we can't do what we love and earn money from it. So, do what makes you happy, and someone will pay you for it. This does not come easy to most people.

Every profession was once thought of by someone and discovered. For example, at first, the profession of doctor didn't exist, but later, someone invented it. There were no designers or engineers. Whatever you have a passion for, someone is making money from it.

It is okay to ask to be paid for what you do because everything in nature is energy, and money is energy too. And since we live in this materialistic world, we need it.

Maybe you have discovered a completely new job that no one has done before. Start doing it and make it a profession from what you have discovered.

Every profession was once started by a visionary, and today millions of people do that job.

So, how do we start doing professional work?

With confidence! I didn't start doing this work for payment either. For years, I didn't earn anything. I invested in myself, but by working with successful people, I stopped thinking logically because I knew that I didn't need to know how it would come. I was inspired by people who themselves wanted to give for what they receive. I live in a place where helping others is well-paid. And today, I have allowed myself to be very well paid for my passion, yet I don't do it for the money. I allow that energy to flow into my life.

Let go of how it will happen, how you will start getting paid. Maybe, from your passion, you start doing it, something that fulfills you, something you would do even without being paid. Follow your passion, and all doors will open because you are in your natural creative flow.

For years, I've been doing this, helping, giving my precious time, and one day, when I started valuing my time, I gave it the highest price. So, all of this had value for me because I was there for someone. So, my time, my energy, my knowledge was in service to someone. This is my passion, but at the same time, it is my work. It is the joy I do with so much love. Forget about logic because logic tells you that you get paid to work, for example, as a salesperson or some other job, because you do it to earn money, and you can't imagine being paid for your beautiful paintings, your wonderful singing, your humor, your sport, and many other passions. Our minds are made to observe, but not to know how something will be done.

Bill Gates, Mark Zuckerberg, Tony Robbins, etc., are people just like you and me. One day, they too started following their passion, and they became who they are today, because no one is given talent for something without a reason.

If the path you are on is beautiful and makes you happy, then don't ask where it leads, just keep walking on that path!

If you live in a way that follows your life energy, it will lead you in the right direction. The path, the lessons you learn from doing what you do or want to do, will feel like a game. You'll do it easily because it is fulfillment for you. A young woman, who had lost her confidence and self-esteem due to the criticism of others, came to me at my office. The voices of others had become her own, and she believed she wasn't worth anything. During our conversation, I realized that she had a dream she saw as impossible to realize now. Because she had heard and seen what some people around her were doing, she thought that was the job for her — to do administrative work.

But on her face, I felt that this job wasn't her passion, it was just an idea from others that she had adopted and was trying to make it her own, thinking that this was the profession she was born for. While talking to her, she told me that her dream had been to become a model. And for the age she was, she thought such a thing was impossible now. But no, everything is possible when we desire it with our soul, when we desire it with our heart, when we have passion and the capacity for it. The impossible only exists in the dictionary of the lazy and the dreamers.

I helped her reignite that desire to live her passion again. Everything takes time, and when you allow yourself to be guided by your feelings and follow the path that gives you satisfaction, you will have the support of the whole universe. This will help you connect with people, get information, and meet someone who will help you live your dreams. Allow yourself to do what you love because it will cost you much to do what you don't love. Don't give your life, your time to something you don't enjoy.

Imagine how much of our life we spend working, giving our time to something we don't love.

FOLLOW THE IMPULSE INSIDE YOU!

A heart surgeon from Zurich had worked for many years in the hospital, but he never wanted to do that work. His true dream was to be a driver, nothing else. One day, he left the job at the hospital and became a truck driver. To some, this may seem crazy, but not to him. Imagine the exhaustion and frustration he had in his life doing work he didn't love. Work without love also has small successes. You can tell through your feelings if you feel tired, sluggish, or lazy to go to work on Monday. Would you have worked all week at that job? Monday is like any other day, but it is the first day of the week, and it shows a lot about whether you go willingly or just because you have to.

Here, you can do exercises, the questions, everything I've given you to find out why you're here, and what you can do to be in creative energy.

One day, I started letting go of all the things, one by one, that hadn't served me. I couldn't do things anymore that didn't bring me joy, so I asked myself: What would I say to myself now if I were 90 years old? And the words started flowing: "Do what you want," "Don't waste time on useless things," "Today might be a year since you started doing what you really want," "Your life is valuable – start following the feeling of fulfillment," "Appreciate every moment of your life," "Your life, your time are the most valuable – don't waste them doing what you don't love." From all of this, I realized I couldn't do anything that I felt wasn't meant for me. Life had a plan for me. With all the experiences I've had, it had prepared me for who I am today. But my decisions to listen to myself and do something different have brought me to understand that this is my passion.

VISUALIZATION

Close your eyes and once again, thank everything that has happened to you, both the good and the not-so-good, because you learn something from everyone and every situation in life.

To lift your emotions, start by thanking life itself. Thank you for your breath, for everyone who is in your life, for all those who have been and those who will be. Imagine that you have woken up in the morning and had coffee or tea, just like you start your day.

Imagine that you are writing and planning your day, and you are happy because now you are going to your office or wherever you work. Start working and feel the satisfaction, feel the love you have for what you do. Imagine you are living your passion. Imagine you are communicating with people or simply working alone with complete satisfaction.

Now imagine someone close to you coming up and hugging you, congratulating you for having the courage to do what makes you happy. Picture all the details of that conversation. If you can't picture it, then imagine you are watching a movie in a cinema, seeing yourself as successful, seeing yourself living your dreams. Feel the emotion, and the more you feel the emotion, the closer you get to the moment when you'll take action in that direction.

Now imagine you are spending time with the people you love and showing them how happy you are, doing what you love, and how your life has taken on new meaning.

Happy people are those who use their talents to the maximum!

The other method I have used is imagining myself at around 85 years old and wondering what I would say to myself if I had the opportunity to motivate myself before life passed by. This exercise has helped me immensely because years pass by, and people think they will live forever. I think of how this person, who is here, has limited time, and we get caught up doing things we think we "should" do. Nothing in life should be done just because of a "should." Over time, I've realized that life is not meant to be lived according to the thoughts and ideas of others about what is good for you. We all have an inner compass that guides us in the right direction. So, the gift you have within you will one day unfold. When I thought about myself being old and asked myself what I would tell Valentina now, I closed my eyes and thought like this:

Life passes by, and now is the time to take that step that you've always been afraid to take. If you don't have a little fear in what you're doing, then even the success you will achieve won't seem that great. So, start with changes in your life because life passes by quickly. You didn't come into this world to live someone else's life, but to live your own. It is yours and only yours, so don't leave it in the hands of others. Only you know your inner world; no one else does, and only you know what is good for you. Others can advise you, but they only know you from the outside, and the outside is meant to do the things that your inner self tells you. It's enough to trust yourself, and the whole universe will help you, guide you in the direction you should go, and show you why you are here. Keep going! Start today to do what you want, what fills you with energy, where you feel that cosmic energy is flowing through you. Start and allow yourself to make mistakes because through mistakes, you will learn what not to do and you will come to understand how things should be done. Allow yourself to make mistakes and learn from them how to move forward.

Life is beautiful, waiting for you to live your legend and unveil the gift you carry within you. Create a high vision, because the higher your vision, the greater you will become as a person. Love and forgive, even when there are stones in your path. Take those stones and use them to build bridges to cross into a better place. Always remember, that even those who try to stop you, are there to push you forward, to make you rise higher, to not stop, and to be happier and more fulfilled. Learn, read, and never say that you know enough, because that will block you from being open to new thoughts and ideas. Never stop serving because that is where the beauty of being human lies. At the moment when you think you don't have the strength to move forward and feel that everything is falling apart, know that everything is falling into place to prepare you for great success, for the next level. At the moment when they try to hold you back by your feet and hands, trying to stop you because they are afraid of you and some don't want to see you rise, free yourself from them and look at your vision. Move forward like an arrow in that direction. At the moment when they applaud you for what you have achieved, tell them that this is just the beginning because they know you can do even more. Life is not about waiting for the destination but about traveling, so the journey is the destination. Keep walking because you are in rhythm with life, enjoy it.

On the day when you think the end has come, go back to the source, go fulfilled in peace, happy because you had the courage to live your life the way you wanted. By doing this, you will have proven to yourself that it was worth being in this life.

Here are 10 affirmations to believe in yourself:

1. I take care of myself.
2. I stay connected to my heart and follow it.
3. I am a light for all those who need my light.
4. I leave my heart open.
5. I choose love, peace, and empathy.
6. I love, accept, and respect myself.
7. I believe in myself.
8. I am a gift to the world.
9. I love myself.
10. Everything I need is within me.

Repeat them, write them down somewhere, and say them until you believe them.

CHAPTER

CREATE A VISION FOR YOUR LIFE!

THOSE WHO HAVE BIG THOUGHTS ACHIEVE MORE IN LIFE!

Believe in unrealistic goals. It's the realistic mind that keeps many people unsuccessful. You are the creator of your own reality, and you can create whatever you desire. I know this may seem very difficult to believe, but it's true. We are the only ones who set limits on ourselves, saying "I can do this much, and no more." Don't forget that nature always supports us and gives us exactly what we ask for. So why not experience and create what we want?

Most people set small goals for themselves because they cannot imagine how a big vision or a big goal can be achieved. But the bigger the goal, the greater the chance of achieving it. Because on the way, you will have small challenges, and they cannot ruin the big goal. They will only prepare you to achieve it. On the other hand, with a small goal, a small problem can distract you from the goal because the goal is smaller than the problem. During the journey, you will face obstacles, and if the goal is not bigger than the obstacles, the obstacles will triumph. However, when the goal is bigger than the obstacles and difficulties, the goal is destined to succeed, no matter how big and numerous the obstacles are.

And it is up to you to decide: will you achieve the goal or succumb to the obstacles? If you reach the goal, you have overcome the obstacles. If you stop at the obstacles, you haven't touched the goal at all. Big goals require big energy, and that energy lies within you. All you need to do is put it to use for your goal. It's like when we're in the middle of the ocean, being hit by waves. Nature has given us limbs to swim, to fight the waves and the fear of drowning and to reach the shore. A person doesn't drown in the sea because they don't know how to swim, because the seawater holds the human body above the surface, even if they can't swim, but because they are overwhelmed by fear, the anxiety of drowning, and death. Therefore, the courage to reach the shore allows us to overcome our fears and anxieties.

Some people don't set big goals because, first, they are afraid of failure or not achieving success. And second, they don't have enough self-confidence and feel small and worthless. They also don't have the courage to dream or to have big goals.

In the universe, there are no limits; you impose limits with your expectations.

Between the person you are now and the person you want to be, there is a gap that, if you don't fill it with self-confidence, it will automatically fill with doubt. Self-confidence makes us great, while doubt makes us small, and to achieve big goals, we must fill that gap between who we are and who we want to be with self-confidence. If we have doubt, then there is an inner contradiction, and we are not motivated to work every day in the direction that brings us closer to the vision we have.

Now go, leave the things for tomorrow, and in doing so, you slowly move away from what you wanted to achieve. If you don't learn, don't take action in that direction, you lose interest.

How to increase self-confidence?

Write down 5 good things you've done throughout the day.

It doesn't matter how big they are; you can write down a kind word you said to someone. Some page you read, something you worked on today for personal growth. It could be a help you gave to someone. The small successes that happened throughout the day, and you do this every day. You will see how your self-confidence will grow, and you continue this every time. Practice and you'll be amazed at how it works. Also, stand in front of the mirror in the morning and say some affirmations to yourself:

For example: Your name, for instance,

Ardiana, you are a wonderful person.
I love you from the heart.
How good it is that you exist.
With your light, you shine on others.
You are a gift to the world.

You can formulate the affirmations however you want or write other affirmations. Practice, write them somewhere, and start believing in them. If at first it seems a bit strange, don't worry, everything is fine. Every time it will be easier to say them, and over time you will believe in them. And truly, words have power, and by writing down your successes throughout the day and doing affirmations in the morning whenever you feel like it, you will gain more self-confidence.

All this will begin to change your perspective because, in the end, you will start focusing on the things you've done well throughout the day, and this will lead you to act in that way again. It's like when you give thanks. The more you thank for the things you have in your life, the more you train your mind to return to the good things, to focus on them, and in this way, your energy will change, and you will have more good things in your life.

There are no limits except the ones we set for ourselves. With the rise in self-confidence, we will allow more to come, and we will allow ourselves to go further. Everything in life aligns with our self-confidence. Having a vision means seeing it internally, in pictures, giving the inner self a picture of what you want to create in your reality. Look for big things and take an album, fill it with pictures of things you desire. Imagine you already have them. Look at how many you can give to your subconscious, feel them, and enjoy them. Don't let others tell you that you can't or don't deserve them.

Seek, and it will be given to you. You are the one who determines how much you want to have, how you want to live, and who you want to be. We make the limits. In the universe, there are no limits. It gives you as much as you want. Therefore, allow yourself.

Ask yourself what you want to create in 3 years... 5 years... 10 years...

The best motivation for a person is to have a magnet, a goal that lifts them in that direction. Goals have an impact on thinking, and thinking pulls you in that direction. That's why it's very important to write down your goals. Because when you write them down, you already have them in your mind, then you record them in your subconscious, and then based on your thoughts and feelings, you take action in that direction. So, with your goals, you have an impact on how your life will look in 10 years. And make your goal so big and beautiful that it becomes a constant motivation, meaning to be motivated all the time.

When you imagine and visualize it, then you get an impulse to take action in that direction. But also ask yourself what kind of person you need to become to achieve the goals you desire?

And don't forget that the journey is more important than who you become, who you meet, what experiences you gain along the way, and so on. Write it down for 3 years and write it in the present.

The law of attraction doesn't know time, and once you have to give it as if you already have it, as if you are living it, write it in the present. And visualize it every day.

Example:

Today, March 20, 2023

I just woke up in the morning and as every morning, I did some exercises, meditated, and now I'm enjoying the moment, drinking a coffee. I am happy and thankful for everything I have, for everyone who is in my life. I have achieved what I wanted, and I am living my dreams. Every day I work on myself to become the best version of myself. And with my change, I change something for the better in the world. I'm doing the work that fulfills me, and with it, I earn money, not only from my passion but also from different sources. I have everything and more money than I need to live. I've allowed it to flow into my life, and the more I have, the more I help others. I have friends with whom I spend beautiful time, I love them dearly, and I am thankful to have them in my life.

I live love and allow it to be free and to be itself. I choose to learn from it and grow together. I live in the house I have desired, decorated according to my style and my partner's. I choose every day to live in peace and love. I choose to forgive, to love, and to be. I am infinitely grateful for the life I live. Every day, my life becomes better and better.

This is just an example to get you closer to what you can write. Write according to your desires, even more. Write in such a way as if you already have them, as if you possess them, as if you are the person you want to be. Read as much as you can and visualize.

Then, you can continue with the other years. I know that at first, it will seem strange, but don't stop and visualize. Visualize as if you've already lived them, and you are at an older age, reflecting on the life you've had. Feel how happy and thankful you are that you have created what you wanted and lived as you desired. Imagine that you thank yourself for working on yourself and consciously creating your reality. Feel it with all your senses, raise the emotion because that is the first manifestation. Imagine you are watching it like a movie, remembering all that you have lived. See yourself achieving them and enjoying. Feel it!

Thank yourself for the courage you've had to be yourself, for taking responsibility, and for the creative energy that has awakened in you.

The one who knows the goal, finds the way!

CHAPTER

MANIFESTATION

For many years, I have dedicated myself to understanding what Albert Einstein, Nikola Tesla, and quantum physics have said.

"If you want to find the secrets of the universe, think in terms of energy, frequency, and vibration!"

NIKOLA TESLA

I started with this quote because it really took me years to understand these concepts and how through our thoughts, emotions, and actions, we manifest. To manifest something in life, you must be in frequency with what you desire. To consciously manifest something in our lives, it is important to keep in mind the pictures of the things we want because everything we see outside has once been in the thoughts of people, and everything exists through the structure of our thoughts. But again, you must know that you have to believe and allow yourself what you have desired. And often, the obstacle is that we are in a state of lack, meaning we seek something because we think we need it to be happy, as we live in the illusion of materialism. I want to give you a very beautiful explanation from Ram Dass about life. He compared it to a clock that keeps ticking. The start is at 12:00, and from 12:00 to 15:00, the person is lost in the world of illusions. From 15:00 to 18:00, the process of de-illusion begins, and then after 18:00, the complete loss of oneself happens, and the awakening of the person starts. It is precisely when a person begins to understand that they are not who they thought they were. I gave this example because you know where you are now, but you are on the path of awakening because you have attracted this book yourself, you have created it with me together.

So, we create together, and everything is connected, and we are connected to everything that exists. And everything is energy.

When we are in the process of awakening, most people turn inward. They spend a lot of time with themselves, meditate, spend a lot of time in nature, and are in solitude. And in solitude, in the depth of our being, we find peace, happiness, and connection with our higher self. A high feeling, an infinite feeling of love, and there we awaken and know our true selves.

I want to wish you from the heart to first be, to know who you are, and then to have. Often, the opposite happens. Many create everything they want, and then they return to a deep understanding of themselves to find and understand their true self, and those things they couldn't find outside, they begin to realize they have them within. Returning to the explanation of how to manifest what we want in our lives. Everyone lives according to their beliefs, their beliefs about themselves and life, and about everything. For example, a millionaire who lives in a mansion, has luxury, and has the art of thinking, the beliefs that have made him live there. While a poor person who is looking for money on the street is not aware that they could create a different reality. They live as they believe and think.

To consciously manifest what you want, I will give you the manifestation tools that I have used to manifest what I have wanted. Just to mention, I have worked with beliefs, with self-confidence, and I have given all of this in this book.

First: Creative Visualization

As children, we used to use visualization, we dreamed, and over time we were told not to dream. And I am telling you today that regardless of your age, where you are, and how you are, dream, visualize yourself as you wish to be, to have, and to do. We do this all the time. We have, let's say, a movie in our minds, but often it is not a positive one.

We all create our reality. I proved this when I started consciously visualizing what I wanted to have in my reality. I visited a friend of mine and saw her in the magazine "Kosovarja." I closed my eyes, visualized myself on the cover of the same magazine, and not only that. I also visualized what they would approximately write about me, and this later happened. Then, I visualized my office, how it would look inside, with furniture, colors, and overall appearance. In some form, through visualization, I had constructed it before it happened in reality. Then, I visualized money flowing, and even though I was in harmony with it, I created it before I started working with people. I also manifested that.

Then I visualized my seminar days in Switzerland. Every detail, and the people listening to me, the music, the meditation, the hugs—everything I saw before it manifested.

I gave you an example of some of my manifestations to show how powerful visualization is.

After I discovered this technique, which, in fact, we unconsciously use every day, I realized and was amazed at how all of this works, and with the power of visualization, I can create life the way I want it.

And with this, I allow myself to be, to have, and to do what I desire, and I listen to my intuition to go where my soul wants to unfold more.

SECOND: ATTENTION AND FOCUS ON THE GOAL

Whatever you give attention to, you give energy to. You give attention to illnesses or things you don't want, and they will manifest more in your life. What you give attention to, you increase it, you nourish it with energy. People do this every day. They give attention to things they don't want, instead of turning their energy toward the things they do want. And by giving attention to them, they create them in their lives.

I know it takes time, but by becoming aware of your thoughts and beliefs, you will start to catch yourself giving attention to the past, to pain, complaints, or things someone may have said today, or things you have heard somewhere or seen on TV.

THIRD: YOUR FEELINGS

We don't need guidance from above because that guidance is found within us. It's the good feelings that tell us we are in harmony with the source of our genius. Follow the good feelings that guide you toward a fulfilled life. Negative feelings show you that you need to turn back because you are not heading where you should be, and you need to change the direction of your attention.

Think again about what you have thought, and you will realize that bad feelings have brought you scarcity, fear, worry. Maybe you allowed these thoughts to come to you unconsciously, and if you catch yourself in these thoughts, then accept it and slowly change your mindset because every thought is creative—it creates your reality around you. And your feelings will precisely tell you which feelings bring you into a happy and fulfilling life.

And I know that bad thoughts show you that you are not in harmony with the creative energy within you, with your soul.

FOURTH: EMOTIONS

They are the driving force behind actions you take because emotion means energy in motion. And they push you to act.

You are responsible for the actions you take to manifest what you want. When I say actions, they come in many forms because deciding and saying yes to something, that too is an action. Start consciously creating your reality.

CHAPTER

THE POWER OF WORDS

Happiness is when what you think, what you say, and what you do are in harmony with each other.
Mahatma Gandhi

You may have heard or read the phrase: change your thoughts – change your life. This is the foundation of absolute change. But thoughts are not enough if the words we speak are not in harmony with our mental state. Change the way you speak because this way may either destroy or build your life. Ask yourself, become an observer of yourself, and listen to what you say every day. The words you speak guide your life toward a quality life or the opposite. Words are expressions of our thoughts and explanations of how we feel. They bring us closer or push us away from people. The best situation is when we are in harmony with all three: thoughts, feelings, and speech. Sometimes we are not aware of what we say because these words come from programs, but I want to help you understand how much power they hold in our bodies. Even when you talk about someone, no matter how you speak about them, you are vibrating that energy and will attract it to yourself. Here, the law of attraction comes into play – you attract what you vibrate. We tend to become the way we think, speak, and act in our lives, and just as we tell ourselves, we create. But often, we are not conscious of the words we choose.

When you say "I can't," you give up control, surrender, and think that you can't control your situation. When you notice yourself in a situation and say you can't do it, simply stop and remind yourself that you always have control and can always choose what to say. A simple example: a friend invites you to a meeting, and the first word you say is "I can't." This word has a low vibration, so you need to change it with another word. For example, “I have something important to do at the moment.” This way, you haven't refused to go, but left room for another time or day.

"I will try"

There is no "I will try." Either you do it or you don't. This is often used by people who are indecisive. "I will try to do it" or "I will try to go" leaves you stuck, making you feel uncertain because you're not saying, "I will do it," but rather, "I will try."

When you say, "I will do it," you send a different vibration.

For example, when your friend says, "See you tomorrow at the café," you won’t say, "I will try." Instead, you will say, "I will be there at that time."

"But" Semantically, "but" is a conjunction that connects two or more clauses in a sentence, usually in a contradictory manner. The second part typically contradicts the first or, in softer terms, disagrees with it. At best, it agrees but offers a different version, either positive or negative, with varying levels of intensity. When we say "but," we automatically disagree with the preceding statement or offer an alternative that we think is better.

For example, if a friend says, "How did the dinner go last night?" and you reply, "It was very good, but it could have been better," you immediately introduce doubt or lessen the strength of the positive response.

Instead, without using "but," you could say, "The dinner was great, and I have a few ideas to make it even better." By using this euphemism, you express your opinion in a way that doesn't make the other person feel bad or create doubt. This approach neutralizes the contradiction and makes communication smoother and more pleasant.

"Problem"

The word "problem," consciously or unconsciously, creates a problem. People immediately associate it with low vibration because it’s linked to something negative. The problem is not the problem; the problem is that we call it a problem.

Instead of the word "problem," use words like "issue," "situation," or "challenge." All three are words with higher vibration and will encourage creative thinking in how you handle situations. For example, instead of saying, "In the future, we'll face many problems," say, "In the future, we'll face many challenges."

"Should have"

We often use this phrase: "It should have been like this" or "It should have been that way." Every time we use it, we are telling our subconscious that we don't have full control over our lives. Stop saying these phrases.

Instead of "should have," use words that make you feel more secure and in control. For example, if someone asks you if you finished a project you were supposed to do, instead of saying "not yet" or "I should have done it," say "I've decided to do it tomorrow." This way, you feel responsible and instill a sense of discipline.

"Difficult"

Often when we want to do something, the word "difficult" comes out of our mouths even before we've thought about it. Without realizing, we are placing obstacles or creating difficulty, often unnecessary, which leads us to think that it's impossible instead of possible. So instead of thinking about what is possible, we prematurely think about the impossible.

We do this not because we see it as impossible, but because we believe it to be so. Before we dare to try, we convince ourselves that it might be difficult. This may seem like a small or insignificant thing in everyday conversation, but if we add this phrase to our daily vocabulary or accept it as an axiom in life, it could complicate things or make our life journey more difficult. Take responsibility for the words you speak, and be careful, as words have power. If you make a mistake, accept it and learn from it. Don't blame or criticize yourself. Say, "Okay, it's fine to make a mistake, I'm human," and keep learning to be mindful of your speech. Be mindful of what you say when meeting someone or complaining. Do you greet with a smile, with optimism, and gratitude, or do you start complaining about how hard life is, how you've had terrible experiences, and nothing is going well? We all know the affirmation and the power of words from former President Obama's phrase "Yes we can." With those words, he motivated millions to choose him as their president. But not many are aware of the power of words and how they speak. Words are creative, they become reality, and if you're not happy with your reality, then be careful how you speak. Good words can break down even steel doors, while bad words can topple the universe.

Be careful of your thoughts, they become words! Be careful of your words, they become actions! Be careful of your actions, they become habits! Be careful of your habits, they become your destiny! Words and thoughts are closely connected to your destiny.

CHAPTER

SPIRITUALITY AND MONEY

CAN WE BE SPIRITUAL AND HAVE MONEY?

You may have heard or believe that being on a spiritual path means you should not earn money. People fear wealth. In reality, they fear themselves and the beliefs they have about money. First, I want to reiterate that everything is energy, and money is energy. It is a means of exchange. In my first book, I wrote about money, but here I want to give a deeper meaning and explain in more detail what it is and how we can allow it to flow naturally into our lives. We earn money by using our energy. I really like the explanations of words in German because they give their meaning, even when divided. For example, the word *VERDIENEN* means "to earn," while the second part of the word, *DIENEN*, means "to serve." So, we earn by using our energy, serving with the beautiful energy we have. We provide service, giving value to others. The more we open ourselves to creative energy, the more we will allow money to flow into our lives. Blockages with money reflect our inner blockages. I want to give all that I have used, which has helped me change my beliefs and financial situation. I have truly said that if I change my vibration here, then I will show others how I did it, because I grew up in a very poor social family, and many times we lacked the most basic things for survival. I've been where you might be right now, but believe me, that reality can be changed because we've been conditioned to perceive situations and not to create them. And my belief as a child was that not everyone could have everything, that there isn't enough for everyone, and many other beliefs that I will write about below, with which you might identify and recognize yourself. Because these are the beliefs you need to work on, and by changing them, your reality will change.

Nothing in this life has meaning except the meaning that we give it. The same is true for money. Through my change, through cleansing, through the work I've done on myself, I have made peace, made peace with the past, changed my views on many things in life, and thus changed my vibration. Money is a topic for many people because many live in a lack of it. I was one of those people, but I tried to understand what money is and how emotions affect their attraction, meaning how the way we view them affects their flow into our lives. Obstacles in paying when we give money make us think we will run out of it. They show the lack we have or the fear of losing it. It is very important to understand that money is energy, just like everything else in the universe. My question a few years ago was: Can we be spiritual, have money, and be happy? And I have the answer. Today, I live all three. I am and I have, but I also choose and decide every day to be happy with how I view the world, with what I've found within myself, and with the deepest feelings of love that I've awakened in myself. To learn about money, it took time and self-work, and I learned from people who understood very well what they are and how to allow them to flow abundantly into our lives. And I asked myself: Why do the rich become richer and the poor become poorer? What's the difference? What do the rich think, and what do the poor think? In the world we live in today, people live in fear of not having enough money, and behind those fears, there are beliefs that block the flow of money into their lives. Many people live in lack, they are in the vibration of lack. But when you understand that we are wealth, we are abundance, we were born to have, we deserve everything from birth, then you will change your beliefs about money. Why do I relate the topic of spirituality with money? Because many people think that to be spiritual and do good to others, they shouldn't allow themselves to earn or receive money. If we don't value ourselves and accept that we already have wealth, our body has no price and no one can pay for it, we have so much, and it is exactly for this reason that we are not very aware, and we live in lack, because we think the wealth we receive from outside is what we need to feel valuable. If we accept our body as complete, as it is, and use the creative energy we have, we become a magnet for money. And when we know that this abundance is in us, we don't seek it from the outside and live completely. We move with this abundance in everything. From my perspective, there are no poor people, but those who do not move fulfilled, those who are not complete. Poverty is a label you have received, which does not exist but is believed to be real. There is not enough, and it is hard to have, and many other beliefs that make you live in lack. If you free yourself from the beliefs you've received from the outside, from your family or society, and now live complete, then your life will transform.

Money is not evil.

Many think money changes a person, changes their beliefs, changes their character, makes them behave differently in society, makes them appear superior to others, but this is not true. Money does not change character, it does not distort personalities.

Money fills pockets but does not enrich the soul, it does not bring love. Money makes people reveal their true faces, those we are used to seeing, whether in a positive or negative connotation. If a person has been poor and appeared to others as good, honest, and kind, and now, when they have plenty of money, they become bad, rude in society, and do not help the poor whose conditions they once experienced themselves, that person was never truly good. Money just gave that person the opportunity to expose their true face and soul. And the opposite, if someone could not help others because they themselves were poor, and now, when they have wealth in abundance, they help others, that person is kind-hearted, and they always were, but now they have the opportunity to show their inner beauty. That person has always been and will remain that way. Money will never change their mind, because their personality was built on human principles, not material ones.

That person will become more beloved, more respected, and more pleasant in both family and society.

Therefore, we should never serve money, but rather let money serve us. Humans have created money, not the other way around. Those who think that money is everything, and who do anything for money, are mistaken. They think that the wealthy are evil and don't want to have their money because they don't want to be bad, but in reality, they just have a belief that blocks them from having money in their lives. They allow themselves to have only what is necessary to survive because they believe that they could become bad.

Some religious books have taught us that we should share our wealth with everyone, give to those who don't have, and in doing so, secure our place in paradise. If money and wealth were truly something bad, people wouldn't have sought to possess them. But they are not to be dependent on or enslaved by them.

But we all know that we deserve wealth because we were born to have everything, to live with everything, but with the beliefs we were raised with, we grow and live by them. And just as universal laws work, we will have the reality we believe in because that's how it will manifest.

Money is neutral, and we make it either good or bad. Money gives us the freedom to express our character, it gives us the opportunity to become who we are, but it's not inherently bad. You can be a good person and have money; you can be spiritual and still have money. I know that it's not easy to change your beliefs about money because they are deeply ingrained, and just as you vibrate, so do you attract. You need to work on your beliefs, seek a different mindset, and allow them to flow. Use your creativity, be in your higher energy, and enjoy. Money will flow from various sources and allow you to have positive beliefs about it and achieve financial freedom. Why can't you? It's enough to work on your beliefs, which I will share in this book, helping you identify which ones you have and transform them. You can take those beliefs and feel them. Do the work you love, serve others, and allow yourself to be paid for what you do because that's how life is: created to live in balance, to give, but also to receive. So, everyone who reads this book, let money flow into your life because it is not bad; it is just as we see it, and as we see it – we feel it, and so we live it.

Does money make us happy?

It is not the duty of anything outside to make us happy. Many people today run after earning more money, buying more things, chasing expensive cars and luxury, thinking these will make them happy, yet they are never content. The biggest illusion of people is identifying themselves with their possessions, thinking that the more they have, the more valuable they will become, boosting their ego by showing off their wealth. But wherever you are, whatever you have, you have your value beyond all that money. Money is simply energy; it's a means of exchange, something we need to give and receive, but it doesn't define who you are. You are not your money, nor your diploma. Therefore, I encourage you to be, accept who you are, and be happy and fulfilled – and then you will also have. I take this as a game. I don't own anything here. I do what I want, and I allow myself to have everything I desire. I've learned to be happy with small things and with little. Learn to be content with what you have. Be grateful, desire more, but don't need it. The more you are in gratitude, the more good things will come into your life. Happiness comes from within, from the way you choose to see life, from how much you love yourself, and how at peace you are in the body you live in. It depends on how self-aware you are. You can be spiritual, happy, and abundant. As Jim Carrey said, "People are happy because they have decided to be happy, and they know that this is an inner job, not an outer one." There is no wrong path, and this is not it either. If you once sought to have, and then saw that happiness wasn't there, and later turned to spirituality to realize happiness isn't in anything external, you can live freely and do good in life. If you think money makes you happy, then why are some of those who have it not happy? They are lost, seeking more to feel happiness, and just keep going, not realizing that the ego doesn't know when enough is enough. The spirit wants to be, and the ego wants to have.

And that's okay. The spirit needs matter to experience itself. Balance is important here in this physical body – to learn to both be and have. You can be spiritual, help others, and accept money.

Some people think that being rewarded when giving something good is a sin or that they haven't done right, and that a simple thank you is enough. Some people think that it's not okay to receive money for the services they offer. They are content with just a thank you. However, a thank you doesn't pay the bills, and it is entirely okay for them to be paid for the energy they give, for the work they do. Therefore, the law of giving and receiving must be respected. Balance is important. Money is just energy, it's a means of exchange. I give you value, help – you give me money. With it, I give and receive something else, and this is how it should circulate. I had this belief at the beginning when I started working with people. I believed that I should work and not ask for compensation. I helped people even when I was busy with children, even after working hours, just to help those in need. I gave so much to others that I started thinking that my time was not being respected. But I was the one not giving my time any value, which they could never return, even if they had all the money in the world. That's when I began to value my time more, and all the investment I had made in myself up to that point. That's when I saw my belief that I shouldn't take something bad for something good I give. Oh, how my eyes opened in those moments. Even though I had made money, I had manifested it flowing into my life from different sources, coming into my account even without working. I still had the belief that I shouldn't take money for the work I did, and there I worked with my belief and was sincere with myself that if I, as a mentor, did this, then I was setting an example for others and teaching them not to respect universal laws. I can give an example of an apple tree. It gives fruit, and anyone can take it, but it also needs the soil, the sun, and the rain to grow and ripen those fruits. Everything serves something, and this is like nature: I give you service, help -you give me money.

So, I began to value what I was giving because I, for one hour of knowledge I was giving, for which I had invested many years, was now giving it to someone ready in a short time. From there, I understood that my knowledge has its value, just as I paid for seminars, read hundreds of books, attended academies, and years I lost working on the secrets of life, discovering all of this to give it to readers in just a few hours in a book. Oh, how much I became aware that nothing is as it seems, but how we see it, we give meaning to everything, and we attract into our lives what we think. Here, I mean for everything in life, and we attract it as much as we believe and as much as we seek. I realized that I must give value to my knowledge and time, and I understood that those who don't value their own time, don't value mine either. But all the lessons I have received, I have learned even from myself that when I paid for something, I received more, so I valued it more.

Change your vibration when you pay or give money!

In everything that begins to change in your reality, you must change the emotion because it is the first manifestation. When I talk about payment, many people, when they give or pay, think they will be left without money.

I am writing this part about money, read it several times because if you make changes here, then your reality will change.

When I came to Switzerland, I saw many opportunities to earn, to have, and at first, we both worked, my husband and I. When many bills came, my first thought was that we were paying too much and very little, or nothing, was left for us to survive.

Be careful if you have this belief because the universal law tells you, "It will be according to your desire." And truly, I lived the reality that I believed, but over time I had a vision and made plans several times before setting it aside and creating a source so I wouldn't have to do the things I didn't want, because at that time, I didn't know what my passion was. Over time, reading and learning, I started to change my belief when I paid and gave money. One day, the children started school, and just like in Montenegro, we bought books, notebooks, pens, and other necessary school supplies. Here in Switzerland, we pay taxes, but we live in a clean, safe place, and the schools organize everything for the children. The tax we paid and thought someone was taking our money was a mistaken belief that many people live with, and they live in lack because of it. I happily pay all taxes, all obligations because I know that these payments are translated into services for the community, for a better life, for advanced healthcare, for higher quality education, a cleaner environment, better municipal services, etc. And all of these, we, along with our children, will enjoy, use, touch, and put into action for good. How wonderful, a completely different emotion. So, I give you the money – you give me the place where I live, I give you the money – you give me the electricity I use, I give you the money – you give me the food, I give you the money – you give me a clean environment. This is where I started to understand this energy, and money started coming more into my life. Even today, I pay, but with a completely different emotion. I am grateful that I live here, I am grateful for everything I have, and I allow it to flow from various sources. Truly, by changing my emotion, my life has changed because that's where the deep belief is, a belief that many of us have, and many of them are negative.

Negative Beliefs about Money

Get your belief that you have, be sincere with yourself because if you don't have it in your life, then surely you have a belief that stops their circulation.

1. Money ruins character.
2. Those who are wealthy don't have true friends.
3. There's not enough for everyone.
4. Money causes division and separation.
5. I feel bad when I have and others are poor.
6. Money is dirty.
7. Money doesn't grow on trees.
8. It's selfish to make a lot of money.
9. You can't have it all.
10. It's too late to make money.
11. Money brings enemies.
12. Only bad people are rich.
13. I don't want to take anything from others.
14. I don't know how to handle money.
15. I feel bad when I give money.

Take the belief you find here or perhaps another negative one you have, write it down and transform it into the one you want to have. For example: I feel bad when I have and others are poor. Transform it to a positive one! I feel very good when I have because with it, I can help those who are poor.

Is it selfish to earn money? Transform it into a positive belief! It is my birthright, to have as much as I want. Work with your own beliefs in this way. I can offer you an exercise to begin building a healthy relationship with money and to start loving it. Keep money in your pocket for one month-at least 50 euros-and do not spend it. Whenever you think or feel that you do not have enough or experience any negative emotion, put your hand in your pocket, touch the money, and say, "I have enough, I feel good with money, I love it, and I allow even more to flow into my life." Say, "I deserve to live in abundance, and money helps me live freely." Ask yourself what your family members or the people you spend time with think about money. Analyze how they live their beliefs regarding money, and you can start to create new relationships and emotions around money.

CHAPTER

LIFE IN ABUNDANCE

EVERYONE LOVES MONEY.

Now you may be surprised because earlier I mentioned the negative beliefs you might have about money, but I want to tell you that deep down, we all love it. Because deep down, we know we deserve it.

Living in abundance means living in your natural state, just as nature is created. In reality, you don't love money as paper, but you love it as the energy that it is. You love the freedom to do what you want and live as you wish. That's why it's important to know why you want money.

For example, when you ask for a lot of money, you want to travel, you want to fulfill yourself and your child's needs, and this is the feeling of abundance. There are many people who are grateful and are in high vibrations, manifesting things without buying them with money, because most people think that only with money can they manifest things, while many things come into their lives without being bought with money. Abundance is the air, health, water, friends, family. If you don't consider these as wealth, as abundance, then you haven't understood how rich you are. Today, someone may die for a glass of water, and this fact can make you more aware of everything you have in your life.

By starting to see the good things you have and being grateful for everything, even though you may think you have nothing to be grateful for, you will train your mind to focus on the good things. Over time, you won't feel the lack anymore, and thus you will vibrate as if you have, you will send the signal that you have, and you will attract even more good things.

Become aware of the abundance around you. Wake up and be grateful for everything you have, and you will become a magnet for more good things. Start giving 10% of your income to others because by doing this, you will tell the universe that you have enough, and this will attract even more.

The formula I have learned, I will give it to you, and it's certain because I used it even before I knew about it, and I realized that I have because I give.

Most people who live in abundance and have money, they give, and they don't give because they have, but they have because they give. Understand the difference.

The formula is like this: 100% - 10% = 200%

I didn't believe this at first either, but in reality, this is how the universe works. We are not separate, and everything we plant, we will harvest. It's well known that you can't harvest without planting. When you give, you're in harmony with nature. You give and you receive, and this is how nature works.

Change your emotions towards money!

Just as you vibrate, you attract into your life. I have mentioned this several times in this book and several times in videos on YouTube. I didn't know that spirituality and money have something in common. We, just as we see them, as we have emotions towards them – we either push them away from us or attract them into our lives. If you don't have a good relationship with them, you don't understand what money really is, and you don't understand why you need to have it.

I didn't understand at first either how important the emotion was that was awakened when I saw a lot of money in someone else's hands.

You can even close your eyes and imagine you have a lot of money in your hands. Notice what feeling arises and discover which emotion is awakened when you hold money in your hand. Again, I'll say that money is just paper with a specific value, and it's a medium of exchange. It's neither good nor bad, but it's just how we see it. And we see it as it is based on the emotions we have towards it, and in turn, we attract it into our lives.

We will only attract as much money into our lives as we feel is good for us. Most people have negative emotions around money. You may notice that those who don't have money speak badly about it. Most of those who don't have it in their lives have negative beliefs about money, and those beliefs affect the emotions we have towards it. Emotions are energy in motion that create the feelings we have for money. Emotions control our minds as they want. Because no matter how much we logically want to attract money, the deep-rooted beliefs, the way we feel about money, are much more powerful. The story we have with money, we defend it and see it as true because we filter it as we believe, and reality confirms it.

I couldn't believe that even from the feeling of being poor, there are individual benefits. Some are poor but don't show interest or work for more wealth. They are content and feel good with what they have.

There are people who want to stay poor to gain attention from others, and that sin is tied to attention. They want attention from other people. Not only regarding money, but people also stay sick for attention from others because they don't love and appreciate themselves.

It took me time to understand all of this, because a person can make themselves sick just to gain attention from others, and talk about illness, poverty, to gain something from it, to have the attention of others.

There are people who use poverty as an excuse for why they can't live the life they want, why they can't achieve their goals or buy the things they want. And for different reasons and beliefs, they prefer to stay without money, they don't want wealth because they want attention, they want justifications, they want to keep their social circle because they believe that money corrupts a person and distances them from society, etc.

I will give you some exercises to change your emotions towards money! Do the exercises because the whole book remains just theory if you don't work with it.

Emotion means energy in motion. To make a change, you need to move, to do something.

1. Write down all the worries you have about money and finances, then choose the three most important ones and reframe them into a positive statement, creating goals from your worries to become a wealthy person.
2. Notice what kind of feeling you have about yourself when you think about money.
3. Imagine people who are wealthy and feel good about it. Wish them well and bless them!

This is a method that has helped me transform harmful emotions into medicine (healing emotions). When I speak of harmful emotions, I say this because it can be measured in people who are full of fear, worry, and negative thoughts. Their blood can be tested and it shows they have poisonous substances in it. Then, with this method, you can use that poison to create something good for yourself. If we try to fight negative thoughts, negative beliefs, we are only strengthening them because we are feeding them. But if we become aware of what we have and work with them, transform them into positive, then we can nourish the positive until our body believes it and reality shows us that we have changed the emotion. If you don't work to transform negative beliefs into positive ones and give them attention and energy, then you will remain in worry, in lack, and you will attract the same thoughts again and act in circles with those tired thoughts. Because the same attracts the same. You feel tired, powerless, humorless, and this applies to everything in life, not just money. Focus your mind on what you want in your life, focus on good things. Focus on the beautiful life you want to live and give energy to it because you are a creator and you create. Name the negative emotion, accept it, and decide to change it! For example, if you have debts, then say: Acceptance - I respect, accept, and love myself even though I have debts and I consciously decide that next year I will have money in my account. And I will see how to do it, I will talk to people who know more about money than I do. Every emotion that we accept, that we have, can then be changed. I also want to share something I realized when I was a child, how the wealthy used to irritate me because I didn't have money for myself. But through all the work on myself during the journey, I realized that if we don't wish for others, then we can't have it for ourselves. Now I understand why this is, because I was vibrating negatively and I didn't allow it into my life. But with the understanding of all this, which I have given in this book, and I wrote it with so much passion, I know that it will change someone's life. Not the book, but the work you will do with this book, because the book will remain mine unless you take what you can use in your life. Every knowledge remains borrowed until you begin to live it, then it becomes your knowledge. I wish and desire for others what I wish for myself. Rejoice in the success of others, enjoy when someone achieves success because all these emotions will be felt by you, and you will send out positive frequencies, and one day, you will be one of those who achieves success.

Wish for what you want to have in life! Not only for money but if you want to have good health, good relationships with others, happiness, then wish the same for everyone who already lives these. Close your eyes and with all your heart, wish for them. Do this and you will see how your emotions will change.

What habits do the wealthy have and what do the poor do?
I will give you 20 habits that wealthy people do differently:

1.They wake up early.
Waking Up Early as a Great Advantage.Thomas Corley spent five years researching the habits of wealthy individuals and concluded that 44% of wealthy people wake up three hours before they begin their workday. I have adopted this practice as well, and in the first hour, I use the 20/20/20 method. To explain, this means: 20 minutes of exercise, followed by 20 minutes of meditation and visualizing my goals, and 20 minutes of listening to a podcast or motivational video. I then write down how I want my day to unfold and create my day. Indeed, waking up early not only allows me to accomplish more throughout the day but also gives me a much higher level of energy.

2. Not Checking Emails or Social Media in the Morning
What does this mean? Why is it important? As I mentioned in the section on creation, what we give attention to, we create. At the beginning of the day, when you are rested, it is best to direct your energy toward what you want to achieve, meditating with your inner joy. First, when the day begins, focus your attention on yourself and avoid immediately diverting

that focus to emails or social media, which could lead you into unnecessary information overload.

3. Eating Healthily

57% of successful people track the calories they consume each day, a practice followed by only 5% of those who are less financially successful. 70% of wealthy individuals consume fewer than 300 calories during breakfast, whereas 97% of those in lower-income groups exceed this amount.

4. Exercising Regularly

Wealthy individuals always find time to take care of their bodies and energy. They engage in physical activities. 76% of wealthy people do aerobic exercise up to four times a week, compared to only 23% of those less wealthy.

5. Having a Primary Goal

Successful people have a primary goal, and they focus precisely on achieving it. According to Corley, 80% of wealthy individuals concentrate on one main goal.

6. Writing Down Their Goals

Goal-setting: Many people want success but never write down their goals for what they want to achieve in life. 67% of wealthy people focus daily on their goals and have them documented, while only 6% of the less wealthy do this.

7. Keeping a "To-Do List"

Wealthy individuals keep track of their tasks for the day. To achieve a large goal, you must take small, daily steps that bring you closer to the ultimate objective. For this reason, 81% of wealthy individuals maintain a "To-Do List," compared to just 19% of those with fewer resources.

8. Believing That Time is Precious

Successful people work toward achieving what they want and do not waste time on social media, as they value their time. They understand that when they waste time on trivial matters, they are losing wealth—the most valuable asset: time—on things that yield no return.

9. Taking Long Lunch Breaks

Many wealthy individuals take long lunch breaks. They know that time is valuable but also understand that rest is essential for returning to work refreshed. They recognize the need to work smart, not hard, and take breaks to stay rested and productive.

10. Reading Extensively

86% of wealthy people read and engage in personal development, compared to just 26% of those less wealthy. They read books on personal growth, and 88% of wealthy individuals read for at least 30 minutes a day.

11. Taking Risks

Wealthy individuals understand that taking risks leads to gains. They are not afraid because they know what they might lose, and they are prepared and willing to take the risk.

12. Networking for Success

Wealthy people know they must associate with successful people in order to achieve success. 79% of wealthy individuals spend at least five hours a month building and maintaining a network of successful people.

13. Knowing When to Stop Working

They understand that when a person doesn't rest enough, they lose productivity, and they do not burn themselves out by working endlessly.

14. Giving

They plant seeds and then reap the rewards. Wealthy individuals give to others and help those in need. Helping others does not make you poor; rather, it results in more wealth. Giving positive energy creates the flow of money and prosperity. When you help others, this action brings fulfillment, happiness, and a sense of love, even from God, as you have extended a hand to someone in need. You are already fulfilled and wish to help others become fulfilled as well. This is truly uplifting and magnifies your sense of purpose.

15. Limiting TV Watching

67% of successful people watch one hour or less of TV, while only 23% of those less successful limit their TV time.

16. Avoiding Reality Shows

Only 6% of wealthy individuals watch reality shows, compared to 78% of those in lower-income groups.

17. Avoiding Gambling

Wealthy individuals do not believe in creating fortune through gambling. They have confidence in hard work and the right strategies to achieve success.

Successful people believe that actions and habits lead people to success and fate, not games of chance.

Games of chance, although they have this name, do not bring you luck. They bring disappointment, stress, depression, waste your precious time, leave you sleepless, separate you from your family, from your loved ones, from your circle and society. They do not enrich you, on the contrary, they impoverish you. They make you spend even the last piece of bread on them. Even the last cents vanish from your pocket and wallet. They make you dependent not only on them but also on many other negative phenomena. The further away from them, the closer to comfort."

18. They have control over their emotions

The rich know that not everything they think should be said. Only 6% of successful people say what they think, in contrast to 69% of the poor.

19. They listen more than they speak

Effective communication is another skill of successful people, and listening is part of it as well.

20. They work longer than others

Most rich people work longer than other people's retirement. The average is up to 70 years. Here, the goal is connected to staying healthy.

People are only distinguished by their habits. With what you feed your mind every day, how you see the problems of life. Do you see them as opportunities or obstacles? What you do, you also feed yourself with. Whatever you engage in every day becomes your life. It is in your hands what you will do after reading this book, but since you have it in your hands, you are on this journey or you have already started. What matters is that you create new habits, new beliefs, and create the life you desire.

Affirmations for a life of abundance

Affirmations are the best opportunity to reprogram our subconscious and thus create differently in our lives. Naturally, it's not enough just to say them but also to give them emotion, to feel what you are saying. Our thoughts, words, emotions, and actions create. The most powerful affirmations are the ones that begin with "I AM," after this, everything we say, we create.

Write or read aloud these affirmations for at least 30 to 60 days.

We are what we think. Everything we are comes from our thoughts. With our thoughts, we shape our world.
(Gautama Buddha")

AFFIRMATIONS

I am a winner.
I am rich.
I am happy and healthy.
Every day, I become better and better.
Every day, I grow as a person.
I live my day consciously.
I am valuable.
I am unique.
I accept that mistakes are important for growth.
I am disciplined.
I am strong.
I am cheerful.
I am a winner because I master difficulties.
I become stronger every day.
I do not give up.
I am courageous.
I am intelligent.
I am wise.
I am...

CHAPTER

SEXUAL ENERGY

The most powerful energy in our body is sexual energy. From this energy, a human is created, life is created. It is life energy. Not only is life created, but through sexual energy, many other things can be born in the human body, such as mental development, creativity, memory, etc.

We have forgotten to dedicate ourselves to life, to our genius.

To be in the present. If we activate these, then we activate sexual energy. Being in the present starts to experience the joy of the moment of life. When we dedicate ourselves to the moment, that beautiful power happens, even when we are with another person experiencing it, it is no longer the thought of orgasm, but simply feeling the body with every breath, meditating. And when you are in the present, you feel this powerful energy flowing through you. In today's time, we have started to give more importance to the body and sexual energy. Some have freed themselves and can speak openly about sexuality, and not only speak but also live it. But very few live it as their body requires because negative beliefs about sex are deeply programmed in every cell of our body. Even though everyone wants sex, they have beliefs that it is a sin to have sex and suppress this energy in the body, this gift from nature. Just like everything nature works to harmonize, the body, like a river that we try to stop, it still finds a way to flow. Sexual energy is natural; it wants to be lived. Sexuality is life energy, and the more we have self-confidence and flow with the energy of nature, allowing all our feelings to come alive, then the life energy flows through us. We feel alive. Over time, some people with their so-called wise minds have written and practiced the idea that this energy is a sin, and even today, many think that such a beautiful and natural feeling can be something wrong. What is natural is not shameful. Sex is not shameful. As a result of sex, we have come into this life. It is shameful and dishonorable not to love something that, thanks to it, we breathe today.

Our life is filled with cosmic sexual energy, and deep inside, we intuitively know that this energy is transformative and creative. Our ego stops us; it is afraid to live it fully. Others have taught us that it is shameful, but they have not taught us that receiving is the lowest energy in the emotional scale. They have taught us to be ashamed of our genitals and to hide them, to suppress sexual energy. Children are told, "It's shameful, don't do that, don't do this," and when a person is programmed unconsciously, they think that it is not good, and thus we grow and suppress this energy. Even today, many people believe that sexual energy is a sin and dangerous. But today, more and more people have started to live it more and let their inner feelings flow. Another thing is that many spiritual people want to separate spirituality from sexuality and do not know that this is the same energy, it is about the same energy. They want to suppress sexual energies to become more spiritual and thus create blockages in their body, going nowhere but to destruction and disharmony. The true nature of sexuality is the nature of the creation of the highest energy, and most people who have achieved success, lived their dreams, have lived this beautiful energy because they have been in their full creative and powerful energy. To start living sexual energy as it was created, we must let go of all the thoughts and beliefs we have about it and trust our body, trust our inner rhythm, to experience ecstasy.

Start to trust this energy and let it flow through your body, live it fully, and you will see how it helps you enjoy the moment in the present. And when you live it, you have stronger creativity, sharper imagination, and are in your greatest universal power.

Through it, human life is created.

With this, the question arises that since life is created through it, is it okay to play with it, to have sex just for absolute pleasure? Yes! Life is created to be a joyful, beautiful game, and all negative contradictions are merely projections of the mind, of the ego. There are many blockages in people regarding sexuality, especially in women. When I speak like this, I do not mean you should necessarily have sex, but you can feel it, experience it in your body, let it pulse inside you, feel alive. In cases where women have been abused or violated, they close their hearts, do not allow love, and in this way, they block the sacral chakra, the sexual chakra, which is connected to the heart chakra, and by closing the heart chakra, they also block the sexual one. This powerful energy is far from what we think about it. When people think of sexual energy, they think of two people together having sex, but it is much more than just what we think. This energy is within us. We can allow this energy to flow within us, and it will have a positive impact on all areas of our life. We begin to shine, we begin to heal ourselves and come into our power. People who use this energy are charismatic, they shine, and they are magnetic to others, to children, to animals. They are connected to nature, like a light that shines on others. This exists in each of us because we are sexual energy, we are created from this energy. The important thing is to begin to live consciously and be aware of every moment where we are. To be inspired, to feel alive and full of energy.

Sexual energy is not only found in the middle of the body but in our entire body. We must know how, through the touch of our arms, face, lips, sexual energy is stimulated. And to activate this energy, it is not necessary for someone else to do it, but for you to come into this energy, you are the person who must come in contact with your body, heal the blockages, and come into this energy. Let this energy flow, use your intelligence, and you will bloom, you will swim in the highest frequencies.

What happens to us when we fall in love?

The greatest part of our lives are the hours in which we have loved.

Wilhelm Busch

The saying that another person completes you and has come to complete you because you are empty, you have gaps, or you are half, has never resonated with me. No one is empty or half. When we fall in love with another person, the most beautiful thing happens to us. That other soul comes to show you your depth, to bring out that which in truth is love. When another person is a strong mirror of you, there is a pull, an intense, strong feeling, and you fall in love. When this happens, cosmic energy flows through you. The other person has come as a channel that shows you the beauty of nature.

Energy flows through us naturally, and we achieve the same enlightenment as people who reach it after a long meditation. These are the deepest and most beautiful feelings that a person can experience. The soul of the person recognizes the other soul, and in the moments of love, you recognize what truly is, as a person should be in love with life, with themselves, and allow someone else to partake in this beautiful energy. You feel alive. The feeling of attraction and intense desire are together and connect in a dynamic energy of life, and all of this is life. Sex is the most beautiful form of expressing love.

Many of us would have liked to keep it throughout life and live this way, but over time, our ego interferes and starts to fade it because it wants possession, it wants to own the other person and begins to recognize the character of that person, not the soul. It begins to see their programs because the soul recognizes differently, and the mind seeks what only it can know. And over time, we become dependent on the other person. We think that person gives us this, but that is the energy that the person has awakened in us, and we have it within ourselves. Over time, this energy gets blocked, and its blooming starts to close before it has fully bloomed. This is because the ego is looking for the fulfillment of its own deficiencies.

The programs we have brought with us from childhood, if we lacked acceptance from our parents, lacked love, and are left with gaps, even though we have fallen in love and surrendered to this beautiful energy, over time, the ego wants those fulfillments, wants those things it thinks it needs to be happy, and with this, it takes advantage and becomes dependent on the other person. Or if someone doesn't love themselves, they wait for the other person to love them, and if the other person no longer loves them, then there is nothing valuable left in that person. To experience love with another person is a feeling that cannot be described. There are signs that show you whether you are truly in love:

- The person you love, you want to have them always near you.
- They are the first person you think of in the morning and the last before you go to sleep.
- You feel very good in their presence.
- Life becomes more beautiful for you; everything becomes more beautiful.
- You have much more energy, and it changes the way you see the world.
- You need touch, and you have a strong sexual attraction.
- Sometimes, you just want to feel them, talk to them, or take a walk with them.
- The small things with this person seem spectacular.
- You care for them, and their health is important to you.
- You share everything with them. Their pain becomes your pain, their happiness becomes your happiness.

I want to say that there is also another kind of love, not only in a person who attracts you sexually. But you can fall in love with a friend or an idol of yours, you can fall in love with the work you do, in which you experience those beautiful feelings, that fulfillment.
You can fall in love with life and everything that surrounds you.

How long does the phase of being in love last?

The phase of being in love lasts from 1 to 3 years for most people. When we fall in love, if we look from a biological perspective, what happens in our body when we fall in love?

It is called the adaptation of chemistry between two people. In the brain, several happiness hormones are released: Dopamine, Serotonin, Adrenaline, and Oxytocin.

All these hormones make us feel happy and energetic, and it's not surprising when we walk with a smile through the city because we feel very good and attractive, we feel full of energy.

To love someone and to be in love with someone are not the same, and when these hormones normalize, then it transitions into love, and now you love that person. Oxytocin ensures that the bond between two people lasts. This hormone is activated when two people caress each other. When both care for each other, take time and nourish that shared connection, showing interest in one another because, in a relationship, there is no plus and minus, but plus and plus. Both are there for each other, to make sense, to be friends, to be together even when things don't seem to be going well, that is, to understand each other.

We can't stimulate chemistry because we have all met someone at some point who did not fit with us. You may have felt that they were not the right person for you. So, this comes from a natural reaction that two people feel for each other.

You cannot force this. The lack of chemistry is the reason why many relationships do not last. A person can fall in love multiple times, but the truth is that once, love can be deeper, making the other person feel in a more profound, different way.

Why does separation hurt?

A person becomes emotionally connected to another and gives part of the responsibility for their own happiness to the other person, not realizing that a person has enough love within themselves and can share this love with the other person.

So, when someone abandons you, they take with them the feeling of being loved, the care and attention they had for you, and at the moment of separation, you feel empty, you feel hollow. Your life no longer seems to have meaning because you no longer have all of those things.

Every time you feel pain, it's because you've moved away from the truth. The truth is that the other person was there with a reason and reflected a part of you. Now perhaps you've learned your lesson, or you may learn it after losing that person because you begin to return to yourself, to work on yourself, and to find that love within yourself. No one in this world is responsible for making you happy.

It's okay to feel loss and pain in the beginning. Don't suppress it! Feel it and let go of that person because, as long as you feel pain, you are still emotionally attached to them.

Many people seek great love, they seek to be loved by others, and it happens. When we find love, we feel we can embrace the whole world. Love should never depend on other people, nor should we exploit others to fulfill our voids.

It's like seeking someone to love you because you don't love yourself. And if you don't love yourself, why should anyone else love you? Why should we expect someone to do something for us when we don't do it for ourselves? Of course, we should love others, but the most important person in our life is ourselves.

The most important relationship is the one with yourself. Whenever we have expectations, we can become disappointed, and we direct that disappointment towards ourselves because no one disappoints us; it's our expectations. Expectations make us unhappy. Where expectations are highest, the disappointment is greatest.

If you want, then love unconditionally, without expectations. Love because you are love and never regret having loved. Because with the love you gave, you've healed something within yourself, and also within the person you loved because it happened for a reason.

We often tell someone "I love you" simply to hear them say "I love you" in return because we are in expectation. We wait for them to give us something, we are beggars. But we are whole, and we are not empty, and we have so much love within us.

Love is not about possession, nor about wanting that love to be sustained by the other person. True love knows how to let go when the time comes. This is true love. It understands that separation hurts, and when someone leaves you, you feel alone, and that's not a bad thing. That feeling is trying to tell you something because it will come back again and again until you understand why it's there. Every feeling carries a message. It's okay to feel sadness. If you feel the need to cry, then cry! Because it has been established that when one person abandons another, in most cases, they experience a huge loss, and if there is dependency, they feel as if they are a drug addict who has left their drugs, or an alcoholic who has left alcohol. Experts have confirmed that it is the same experience in the brain. The love you are constantly seeking outside, it waits to awaken within you through self-acceptance, through healing emotional wounds. This love has been inside you all along. God loves you, and every time you move away from this feeling, you feel pain. This is the message that it's not supposed to be like that. You are already loved unconditionally, you are accepted, and you are special. Some people come into our lives to help us grow and understand the truth. Afterward, when we are healed, we must let them go and allow them to continue on their journey.

Heal your pain, be love and light, and spread this love to others because by giving, you will have more and more. There is an inexhaustible source within us.

Most people feel like no one will love them, but sometimes they need to experience what is not love in order to create true love.

This is life, but most people, even themselves, don't take the initiative to leave someone because they don't want to hurt them. But just think for a moment: if you are sincere with that person and tell them you can no longer live with them, or be in a relationship with them because you don't love them anymore, then that person does not care about how you feel; what matters is the feeling you give them. Then think again: do you really want to be with that person? Because a person who loves, knows how to let the other person go, because they do not only care about their own feelings, but also about the other person's well-being, and allows them to go on their own path and future journey. People suffer because they don't go to what they have perhaps created with that person. You must ask yourself, "Am I the one who is dissatisfied and have I made myself a victim of the partner, seeking someone else?" Then you must work on yourself to come to your own love, to be complete within yourself, and then share it with others. If someone no longer resonates with you, then you have done enough and created other things. But if this is not the case, you will feel that person's presence, and you will have created something completely new.

Now learn to let go, to free yourself, and to be in harmony with yourself. Learn to let go of people who take your breath away. Those who do not allow you to be yourself and to do what you want, because a healthy relationship is one where two people do not use each other to fill the other's voids, but where they have the freedom to be themselves. When they can live without a partner and still choose to stay together, that's what I call a healthy relationship.

Someone will love you as you are, even if you have some physical flaws or imperfections. Exactly with those so-called flaws that you think you have, or perceive as obstacles for someone to love you, that's precisely how someone will love you. Just as you are.

In pure and genuine love, there are no flaws or weaknesses! The flaws, imperfections, and weaknesses in love disappear when the relationship fades, when feelings fade, or when they are extinguished entirely. After that, to find a reason to separate, negative aspects are sought (while erasing the positive ones) to justify the departure.

If you love someone let them go! If they return to you, then it is yours forever! Confucius

CHAPTER

CHILDREN

We should not lose the way children see the world. For me, the greatest spiritual teachers are children. They teach us to live in the present, to feel our emotions, to be in the now, and not suppress anything. They teach us to accept and love ourselves as we are. They teach us not to give up on anything we desire in life. They teach us to be creative. That's why, for me, there is no greater spiritual teacher than children. They are pure energy coming from the source. They are closer to the source and are pure, clear beings. They know who they are and why they are here. Parents are there to help children develop physically, intellectually, and in terms of their personality, while children are here to remind us of our intuition and depth. They help us reconnect with God within ourselves. We are not the owners of children; we are a channel through which children come to us. Since we have not yet seen for ourselves who we truly are, most people think that children don't know anything and see them as small because they are physically so, and intellectually they assume they don't have enough responsibility and are not very conscious. Children need us as an example in the physical world of how to live positively and constructively. If we do this, they imitate us as parents. Children have a high capacity for attention. They don't do what we say, but they copy us as we are. Through your transformation, through your change, you will have a great impact on the children because they will gradually adapt to your energy. If you see how much they reflect us, the things we have within ourselves, you will be amazed. If parents behave in a way that they don't express what they feel, children will express exactly those emotions that the parents have suppressed. They are sincere, truthful, and they don't know how to hide what they feel. The reaction of children can help us process our own suppressed emotions. If you act a certain way in front of children as though you're fine, but inside you're stressed, they will react to the energy you are transmitting, not to how you try to appear. So children reflect exactly what you are feeling in the moment.

This has happened to me, I've done the same thing in the beginning of my work, that's why I speak from my experience. I believe children should not be educated this way, to act like robots, not showing their emotions, especially when they are told, "You shouldn't cry because you're a boy," and when they grow up, they become cold, closed-off individuals, and have blockages. Tears are good; they are a release of emotions, and we shouldn't stop them. We need to cry when we need to. Nature takes care of us when it's time to cry, release, or be joyful and laugh.

Imagine a glass that is full of water, and you pour more water into it; it spills over. That's what happens with the body. It can't hold onto it, and it becomes a blockage for the natural flow of energy in the body. It is Necessary to Release That Blockage. In the West, there is a prevalent belief that children should grow up without any negative emotions, but this actually harms them because they are told that the emotions they have are not good. And people start from originality and then become copies of something others expect from them, and in fact, most people die as copies and don't work on themselves or don't allow children to be original as they are. If they have an emotion, they should express it and live it. By allowing them to experience all emotions, they will become wise over time. That child will accept themselves as they are and will not criticize themselves. They will know that all emotions are a part of life. What I am not saying here is that you should vent your frustrations and anger onto your child, but you should be sincere. When you're not okay, show that you're not okay. Don't hide those emotions, because that teaches the child that their emotions are not okay, and then they also think that they are not okay, creating blockages within themselves. But even if you do it sometimes-if you behave in an inappropriate way and release your emotions on them-then learn to apologize and show them that you also make mistakes and that mistakes are human. Forgiveness is great!

Teach your child to take responsibility as early as possible!

The sooner you teach them to take responsibility for their life, the sooner they will learn to live as a winner, as a creator of their own reality. One mistake that many parents make is taking on the responsibility for their children and becoming victims. They forget themselves while trying to do everything for their children, and in doing so, they victimize their children as well because they learn that someone else has to take responsibility for them. This makes them dependent on someone, and as such, they also become victims. Children learn from examples. If you are in your own energy, love yourself, and the most important person for you is YOU, you will teach your child to do the same. Don't forget, children don't listen to you; they observe how you are. The happier you are as a parent, the more you teach and transmit that happiness to your child, especially when you show the child that no one makes you happy, so you don't use your child for your happiness or to fulfill your own unmet needs. You help them stay in their own energy the way you are in yours. I have met many mothers who feel guilty because they work and haven't spent much time with their children. What I want to say is that there are many mothers who stay home and think they have their child close. The child needs examples and love; they learn the rest from their own experiences. If you give up on yourself and become a victim, forgetting yourself to be available 24/7 for the child, this not only harms you but also your child, because they will feel oppressed by excessive care and control. Children need to be allowed to be themselves, to try, to learn, to fall and rise on their own, and to learn from their own experiences. In this way, you should be there as a mentor, to help them with love in their journey and your shared journey.

Children, until puberty, live on the energy of their parents. Unconsciously, they take in the emotions of their parents, even those that the parents don't express.

Thus, it is essential that parents be well, as it is only in this way that children can do things for themselves, to educate themselves, and to strengthen their physical energy. Children bring with them everything they need. They possess everything within themselves, each having their own inner compass to guide them. They come without a sense of time, with all their creativity, and without fear. Learn to allow the child to be as they are. When I speak in this way, I mean that the child does not need your education or for you to impose your beliefs and programs on them, thinking they are good. Live freely, listen to your own feelings, be present and ensure that your actions align with what you feel. In the same way, teach and allow your child to do the same. Step away from the logic that you know everything, from the belief that what you know is the best, and from imposing your views on your child. It has been observed that children who are not allowed to be themselves, but rather forced to adapt to their parents, grow up unhappy. Here are some tips to help your child feel whole, good, and secure, just as they are. Allow them to be themselves.

1. **Give love!** Hug them, be there to offer warmth and love. Again, turn inward, ask yourself what your own needs are, what you need to give yourself, perhaps the love you never received from your parents. As I mentioned earlier, many parents do things for their children based on their old patterns, their own deficiencies, acting from what they think are gaps within themselves. Always turn inward to understand what you need; what thoughts make you feel whole, happy, and allow you to transmit that to your child.
2. **Understanding how to communicate with your child:** Speak gently and understand the emotions they are feeling in the moment. Thus, communication between you and your child should be clear, empathetic, without criticism or judgment. If the child has a request and you cannot fulfill it at that moment, talk about your feelings; don't act against yourself. Allow your child to understand you in a way that helps you understand them as well.
3. **Respect your child!** Respect, like everything else in life, is a reflection of what we give. Think about this—if you believe you are the more mature one, have more experience, and think that your child knows nothing, and if you fail to respect them, treating them as your property or venting your frustrations on them, eventually the child will understand that they are a separate personality and will only respect you as much as you have respected them. Therefore, the respect of your child must be earned. I often use a method, especially with other children, where I kneel down to speak to them, making eye contact, rather than

speaking from above or looking down. I do not make them feel inferior because they are not.

4. **Let your child be free!** I know this is not always easy, but it is the most important aspect of a child's development. Let your child say, "I do everything that benefits you and others." Let them take out all the kitchenware. Understand that children need to touch more than 100 things in a day to strengthen their creativity. Understand that the early years are crucial for children to learn to live in their physical bodies. This is a very important time when people internalize beliefs and programs telling them they must listen to others, not their own feelings.
5. **Give your child time where time doesn't matter!** Here, I suggest allowing your child to do things that might seem like a waste of time. After all, children, up to a certain age, do not have a clear sense of time. But today, in the modern era, they often start daycare early, then school, and their lives are highly structured. Allow your child time to play and do things where time is not a concern. This time is crucial for fostering creativity and imagination. It is a significant period for their development.
6. **Affirmations**: Every criticism you offer a child will eventually be internalized and repeated by them, often becoming their belief, and they will become how they think about themselves. Speak positive affirmations to your child daily, give them strength, tell them how wonderful they are, and let them know that it's okay to make mistakes, as they learn from them.

Tell them they are beautiful,

Tell them they are good as they are,

Show them that they are a wonderful child.

Let them know you are grateful for their existence,

Tell that you trust them, and that you enjoy their work.

Remind them that everyone makes mistakes, that they are courageous, and that they are a gift to the world.

This does not mean we ignore the things children do during the process or accept everything. We need to be sincere and show them when something is wrong, teaching them how to do it differently, especially helping them understand the cause and consequences in life.

Children observe; they do not just listen.

The way you treat people, nature, animals, and yourself-your child watches and takes example from you because you are their first leader in life. You are their primary mentor. For the benefit of the next generation and for your child's well-being, you must be a role model. You must educate yourself and be authentic, be yourself, and work every day to become the best version of yourself.

Embrace Calmness and Live in the Present!

One day, some people came to a wise man who was alone and asked him, "What meaning do you give to the life of stillness and meditation?" The man was looking into the depth of the water and said to them, "Look into the water, what do you see?" They looked into the water and said, "We see nothing." After a short time, the wise man asked them again to look into the water. "Look into the water, what do you see now?" "Now we see ourselves," said the people. "While I was looking at the water, it was unclear, and now it is clear." This is the experience of stillness and meditation. You see yourself, just wait a little longer! "What do you see now?" asked the wise man. They looked into the water and said, "Now we see the stones at the bottom of the water." This is the experience of stillness and meditation. If we wait long enough, we can see the depth of everything. Often we think that we have enough time for something, and we are in a rush. We are somewhere, but not here, in this moment, and we don't live consciously. We do not stop to become aware of the moment. When we are with a person, we see that in every person there is something magnificent. How many moments do we waste being upset over trivial things? We lose life worrying about things that never happen. Thus, by not being in the present and thinking about the past or future, we experience different movies that are perhaps not even good movies at all. I know that our nature, our brain is designed to protect us, but most of the fears and negative thoughts come from the programs we have received. "Beware of this, this will happen..." And so we spend most of our time in stress, in fear, which is not happening at the moment; they are only thoughts. When we begin to become aware of the present moment, we will start living truly. We will become like children, we will be happy, we will laugh, and we will experience beautiful moments by experiencing the present where life is. We only have this moment.

In stillness lies the power!

Confucius

When you have a moment where something makes you feel bad, ask yourself after 5 years if this situation would bother you, and return to the present moment. Be aware of your breathing, your body, and focus on something good. Be thankful for life, for what you have, and you will feel better. The moment now is the only one we truly have. We will always be in the present. Right now, when you are reading these words carefully, your life is happening. Now, you are living in the present. As soon as you start thinking about the past or the future, you stop living in the present, where life is. After many years of meditation and self-work, I began to return to the feeling of being like a child, and somehow I was amazed. I asked a wise person who, in different parts of my life, helped me understand those things that happened to me, and I am very grateful for how nature connects me with such people. It took me time to learn to become aware of the moment, to stop time, and to have my full attention on one thing. Even when I went outside, I saw flowers, trees, things I hadn't noticed before because I was somewhere else, not in the present.

Why do I share this? Because I want you to know that many people live but are not truly living because they do not savor the present moment. I asked that wise man if I was doing well. I began to appreciate small things: being happy, picking flowers, listening to birds chirping, feeling the light breeze, the rays of the sun, hearing the sound of water, and like Pippi Longstocking(movie character), I danced down the street, wondering whether I was crazy or what was happening to me. He laughed and told me that this was my achievement. I asked him if I had meditated for all this time and read all those books for this. He said yes. I was amazed at the fact that to live in the present, we are alive, we have energy, we don't have worries, and we don't give time to the past. In fact, we are truly living. It's like a child who plays and doesn't know how much time has passed because they are completely there, and time doesn't matter. For years, my mind searched for the secrets of happiness, and after all that time working on myself, I returned to the realization that life is very simple. Life is beautiful when we begin to live more in the present.

I know that at first, it might not be very easy because you spend most of your time in the past and feel depressed about what happened, and then you try to bring yourself to the present. The pains of the past disturb the present moment. But with this book, I want to raise your awareness and wake you up to understand that you can change your perspective even about the past. Realize that everything was there to give you a lesson, to help you create something new today. By taking responsibility for how you will view these experiences, you will close the page with everything. You will take the lesson, and it's okay to write the life you want to have, to make plans, to see the future as you want to live it, and manifest the things you want in life, but don't spend your life being somewhere else. So, live more in the present.

When you walk, become aware of your movements, your voice, your breath, the birds singing, etc. Be present and listen when you are in a conversation—what is the other person saying? Listen carefully and be present. When you are with those you care about, feel the hug, give time to that person, be there with them and not somewhere else with your thoughts. The beauty of life is in the present, no matter where you are. Even in the shower, when you are there, feel the water flowing through your body. Be a spectacle in the moments where you are. Enjoy the little things. Make your life have beautiful moments. We don't always need to do something; sometimes, we just need to be. The secret of happy people is that they take the moment as a miracle and are thankful for being truly present.

CHAPTER

LIVE IN HARMONY WITH THE UNIVERSAL LAWS!

7 UNIVERSAL LAWS

How does our life work?

All these laws give us a truth in hand, showing that we are the creators of our reality. These are natural laws, known only in depth to a few. Spiritual teachers like Deepak Chopra, Rhonda Byrne, Louise Hay, Eckhart Tolle, and many others have given teachings based on these laws. Not only these teachers, but even religious books are based on these laws. Along with all those physical laws, we also have the laws of consciousness (awareness). Just as gravity works on Earth, so do these laws, even though we are not always conscious of them. By using these laws, we can have a different perspective on life, create consciously, and understand the lives of others as well.

William Walker Atkinson was the person who dealt with these laws and brought them together in a book called *The Kybalion*, presenting them in a simple way to explain these laws. Before I had information about these laws, I lived unconsciously and was always influenced by external circumstances. My life was a constant battle with the outside world, and I didn't realize that the battle was within me, only reflecting my inner struggles. People would come into my life who treated me poorly, and I didn't have good relationships with others because I was battling within myself, and every day my fears and frustrations grew as I fed them.

From the moment I started to realize that there was more to life than I had known, I began to follow spiritual teachers, learn from them, and especially started going within myself to see what was there. I began meditating and, every day, I understood more about these laws. And these are what I want to share with you. If you use these laws in your life, you will start to understand much of what happens. You will be able to change your energy and begin creating what you want.

By first working with the Law of Attraction, one of the universal laws, I began to understand how powerful we are. When we start consciously using these laws, an incredible power within us is unlocked. It depends on your level of awareness how you will understand and whether you will completely grasp these laws. Maybe one law will be clearer than another. As will be shown in the explanation of the laws, nothing happens without reason. So, even this book is not without reason in your hands. Therefore, return to these laws because they are laws that will never change in your life. They have been, are, and will remain for life.

The 7 Universal Laws are:

1. **The Law of Mentalism (Creation)**
2. **The Law of Vibration (Movement)**
3. **The Law of Correspondence**
4. **The Law of Cause and Effect**
5. **The Law of Polarity**
6. **The Law of Rhythm**
7. **The Law of Gender**

THE LAW OF MENTALISM (CREATION)

The Law of Creation is the foundation of Hermetic philosophy, upon which all other laws are built. It states that everything is spiritual in its origin. In other words, everything is energy. The material universe that we can see and touch is the effect of thinking; it is the cause of our thoughts. Everything that has been created started with a thought or an idea. A thought becomes matter. A negative mind cannot have a positive reality. The reality that we see is a reflection of our thoughts and beliefs.

With our thoughts, we create our reality.

For example, a house is not built just by chance. A person first has an idea, then creates a plan, and begins the construction. Then, the thought becomes a reality. Through thoughts, emotions are created, and finally, actions are aligned with the thoughts and emotions.

How can we make a positive change with this law?

Instead of looking for change outside of yourself, you must go to the core within yourself to change your beliefs and thoughts about something. The world adapts to how you perceive it. Therefore, to change your thoughts, you must first change within yourself, and this is what many teachers have said: If you want to change the world, first change yourself.

THE LAW OF VIBRATION (MOVEMENT)

Nothing rests; everything moves; everything vibrates.

Kybalion

In other words, everything we perceive as matter, at the energy level, is in constant movement. Everything in the universe is made up of energy that vibrates. Every person, with their thoughts and emotions, vibrates, and as they vibrate, they attract their life experience. Just as we feel, that is our vibration-either low or high. If we have negative thoughts such as fear, anger, resentment, sadness, etc., these are low vibrations, and we may feel heaviness in our bodies. On the other hand, thoughts such as happiness, gratitude, love, are high vibrations, and we experience them as lightness.

We can consciously change the vibration of our bodies by altering our thoughts and emotions. This phenomenon is also known as the Law of Attraction. The emotion associated with something is more powerful than the thought because the heart has a magnetic field 50,000 times stronger than the brain. This is why many people cannot change their vibration just with thoughts because those things that are registered within you vibrate differently and are much more powerful. Emotions vibrate and attract those similar vibrations.

Be the energy you want to attract into your life!

You need to deeply believe in your heart that you have it, see it, or live it now, and you will begin to change your emotions and thus your vibration. All you need to do is bring yourself into the frequencies that align with what you want to create in your life. If you want love, then give love. If you want to live in abundance, then be thankful and feel yourself in abundance. Everything in nature is vibration. Everything has a frequency. Every thought has a vibration, every feeling has a vibration, and every action has a vibration. You can only receive the vibration that you send out. You cannot be in a low vibration and expect to have a positive life. If you want to attract different things into your life, you must change your body's vibration.

THE LAW OF CORRESPONDENCE

As above, so below; as below, so above.

Kybalion

The Law of Correspondence teaches us that everything we have inside of us is reflected outside, and what is outside reflects back into us. The beliefs we hold about something, situations, or people will always be mirrored back to us based on the beliefs we carry within. This connects to my favorite quote from Dr. Wayne Dyer: "When you change the way you look at things, the things you look at change." So, just as we see things, they reflect back to us, and if we want what we see to change, we must change our perception -in other words, change our beliefs.

If we give love, happiness, and positivity in life, that is what we will attract. If we give hate, pain, fear, and other negative things, those are what we will receive in return. If we expect things outside of us to change in order for us to be happy, then we will continue to wait. You must change within for your external reality to change. Everything is as it is. We are the ones who assign meaning to life, events, or situations, and make them either negative or positive.

Most people do not want to look into the mirror of the outside world and see what is within them. They do not want to accept that the things they oppose outside are also within them. The good or bad things that reflect back into our reality have something to do with us, because otherwise, we wouldn't see them.

The Story of the Law of Correspondence

Many years ago in India, there was a temple with 1,000 mirrors. It was located high in the mountains. One day, a man climbed up there and looked at the temple with the 1,000 mirrors. When he arrived, he was afraid, and as he looked at the mirrors, the 1,000 reflections all showed the same fear and anger he had inside. Panicked, he left the temple, thinking that life outside was dangerous and full of threats.

Not long after, another person went up to the temple. When he arrived at the mirrors, he saw many reflections of people smiling and playing joyfully. This man left the temple happy, knowing that the world was full of happy and kind people.

What does this story tell us?

It shows us the meaning of the Law of Correspondence. When we behave with others in a positive way, the positive energy returns to us in the same way.

THE LAW OF CAUSE AND EFFECT

"Every cause has its effect; every effect has its cause."

Kybalion

The Law of Cause and Effect teaches us that everything that happens has a cause, and everything we experience is the result of a cause. Nothing happens by chance or coincidence. In life, there are no random events; everything is connected through these laws.

As we say in Albanian, "What you sow, you shall also reap." This reflects the idea that our thoughts, emotions, actions, and decisions all contribute to what happens in our lives. If you think negatively, this is the cause, and the effect will be a negative life. You cannot think positively and have a negative life, and you cannot think negatively and expect to have a positive life.

Everything that exists today was once a thought.

Everything you see and experience is the result of how you thought, felt, spoke, and acted. This fact might be frightening for some because they may realize that some of their past thoughts or actions may not have been ideal. However, the good news is that you can change your life today by applying these universal laws.

Although it is not easy, because 95% of our thoughts are unconscious, and it's difficult to control them, with awareness, we can slowly begin to plant the seeds of the life we want to live.

THE LAW OF POLARITY

"Everything is dual; everything has poles; everything has its pair of opposites."

Kybalion

The Law of Polarity tells us that everything in the universe exists in pairs of opposites. These opposites are simply different degrees of the same thing. There is hot and cold, light and dark, good and bad, up and down, and so on. These polarities are part of a greater whole, and without one, the other wouldn't exist. For example, there is no such thing as "cold" without "heat." The concept of cold can only be understood because we know what heat is. Likewise, light is only recognized because of darkness. The two opposites are part of a continuum, and they complement each other. This law also implies that within every challenge or difficulty in life, there is something positive or beneficial. If you're facing something difficult or unpleasant, you must remember that this moment, no matter how hard, contains within it something good, even if it's not immediately apparent. Even though I couldn't see the good when I was facing illness or hardship in the past, I now understand that those experiences had something valuable to teach me. I'm now grateful for the challenges and suffering I've gone through because they taught me life lessons that have made me stronger.

So, when facing difficult situations, try to maintain your patience and belief that this moment, no matter how tough, is happening for a reason and may ultimately lead to something good. Remember, every challenge carries within it the seed of something better.

THE LAW OF RHYTHM

"Everything flows in and out; everything has its tides; all things rise and fall; the pendulum swings in one direction, then the other."

Kybalion

The Law of Rhythm explains that everything in the universe is governed by cycles and rhythms. From the cycles of nature (like the changing of seasons) to the rise and fall of emotions, everything moves in a predictable pattern, with highs and lows, beginnings and ends. Life is a constant motion of ebb and flow, just like the swinging of a pendulum.For example, we can observe the cycles of life, such as birth and death, day and night, and the changing seasons. These rhythms are inherent in the fabric of existence. In our own lives, we experience moments of joy and sadness, success and failure, peace and chaos. These ups and downs are a natural part of our rhythm.

Buddha once said, "I have learned that everything is constantly changing." This is a reminder that both pain and pleasure are temporary. They come and go. So, even when we experience hardship or difficulty, we can take comfort in knowing that these moments are not permanent. They too shall pass.

We must also remember that every experience, no matter how challenging, is part of the natural rhythm of life. Everything is in constant motion, and this rhythm guides us through the highs and lows, teaching us lessons along the way. Even when it seems like nothing is changing, the rhythm of life is still at work, bringing about transformation.

The key takeaway is that we should not be discouraged by the inevitable ups and downs. Embrace them, knowing that they are part of life's natural cycle.

THE LAW OF GENDER

"Everything has its masculine and feminine principles."

Kybalion

The Law of Gender explains that every aspect of the universe embodies both masculine and feminine energies. These energies are not related to biological sex but to spiritual and energetic principles that exist within everyone. Both men and women carry these energies, though their expression might differ. In this context, the feminine energy is often associated with intuition, wisdom, receptivity, and creativity. It is the part of us that receives and nurtures ideas, feelings, and dreams. When we neglect this feminine energy, we may experience imbalances in our lives, and it may try to express itself through dreams or emotions. It's the source of higher wisdom within us, trying to guide us if we are willing to listen. The masculine energy, on the other hand, is associated with action, logic, thought, and movement. It is the energy that brings things into physical manifestation and executes plans. Every individual, regardless of gender, has both energies. The masculine energy actively takes the ideas or inspiration received from the feminine and puts them into action in the world. Together, these two energies work in harmony to create life, change, and progress. In many cultures, this is symbolized as "Yin" and "Yang" in Chinese philosophy, where "Yin" represents the feminine (receptive, nurturing) and "Yang" represents the masculine (active, dynamic). To live in balance, it is essential to honor both the masculine and feminine energies within us. When these energies are in harmony, we experience creativity, flow, and purpose. If one energy is suppressed or ignored, it can lead to imbalance in our physical, mental, or spiritual life.

By integrating both energies, we tap into our full potential and are better able to navigate the world with wisdom and action, understanding that both receiving (feminine) and doing (masculine) are essential to our overall well-being and creative power.

For example:

A mother may experience an intuitive moment where she feels that her child is in danger. This feeling comes from her feminine energy, her intuition, telling her that she needs to intervene. She rushes into the kitchen and stops the child from burning his hand. This is an example of the interaction between feminine and masculine energy. The feminine energy gave the feeling, while the masculine energy expressed itself through the action.

When these two energies work together, the individual creates a creative life and lives in harmony and positivity. This can also be explained by my personal experience, where my intuition guided me to do something, and the action I took was based on what my intuition had given me. This is a collaboration between feminine and masculine energy, where intuition (feminine) and action (masculine) come together to bring positive and creative changes. I have experienced this feeling when I listened to my intuition and acted in alignment with it. After that, I felt high energy, love, peace, and wisdom flowing within me. This is a natural process when feminine and masculine energies are in harmony and work together to bring more light and balance into our lives. In many cases, people have used only masculine energy, focusing on thoughts and actions, and trying to have everything under control. This can be called the ego, and when this happens, the person loses connection with themselves and creates an internal imbalance. When a person identifies only with their achievements, their wealth, or how many followers they have on social media, they have moved away from their true self. They have lost touch with feminine energy, which is the source of peace and wisdom, and have replaced it with ego and control. The mind is creative, and we should not identify with it. When we allow the mind to create and let the feminine and masculine energies cooperate, we reach a complete harmony, creating a balanced and fulfilling life.

CHAPTER

LIVE IN THE LIGHT

For many, many years, the Lords believed that it would not be beneficial for people to quickly discover all the wisdom of the universe while they were still not mature enough. Thus, the Lords decided to conceal wisdom in a place where it would not be easily found until people were prepared for it. One of the Lords suggested hiding it in the highest mountains on Earth. However, it became clear to the Lord that humans would ascend even the highest mountains. Another suggested hiding it at the bottom of the sea. But even there, it was thought that wisdom would be quickly found. Then, the wisest of all the Lords spoke: "I know what we should do. Let us hide the wisdom of the universe within human beings. They will only find it when they are ready, for to find it, they must return to the path that lies within themselves."

With this story, I wish to convey that all wisdom resides within you. To find your inner wisdom, you must be willing to explore your own depths and connect with the light you carry within. Living in the light will illuminate all the darkness you have known until now. Your life will shine, and you will truly become aware of yourself. All that we think we are, we are not. For when we know who we truly are, we cannot explain it by what we think we are.

When we reach our true self, we realize we are light, interconnected with all existence. At our core, we are all the same. The light itself does not know it is light, just as it would not have known to seek to live its opposite. We come into this life as souls, knowing all that we are, yet in this physical form, we possess a mind that gives us the illusion of another self-what we think we are.

Thus, the Spirit or Light comes, is reincarnated (incarnated) into a body and mind, to experience the lessons it has come for. When it comes, it forgets all of this, to embrace the journey. Why is it said that all is found within us? To understand this, one must know that all wisdom is found within us. We learn, we are educated, we adopt new habits and thoughts, we live as we wish. Yet, wisdom and all knowledge reside within us. What is outside of us serves only as a reminder of what we have always known.

To live in the light means knowing who you truly are, to live in love and use your mind-not to identify with it or with what you think you are. Living in light means choosing to live where it is easiest to be, to be understanding, to be forgiveness, and to be a source of all good. And the ego must be understood and befriended, for even the ego has its purpose. Many spiritual teachers wish to eliminate the ego, but in doing so, one fights ego with ego. The ego is with us for a reason. The spirit knows why it has chosen the ego, so why do you attempt to eliminate it with your mind?

The task is to create balance between these two aspects. To know you are spirit and to use the ego, to make peace with it. I cannot explain all that I have experienced, but from the moment I understood who I truly am, everything changed in my life. There is no more division, no more judgment, no more blame. Everything has transformed, and all fears have vanished. I cannot explain it because our rational minds are limited. If anyone can explain it, they have not truly understood it because there is no explanation—this must be experienced.

Carry the light for the world.

Tell everyone, fear not;

God loves you and all of humanity.

For you are love, you are light. Carry light for the sick, for the children, and for the elderly. Do not abandon them, for you are love and light. I wish for you to see the light you carry within yourself, to understand that what we thought we were until today is but an illusion we created to test ourselves and prepare for the gift that our spirit came here to unfold.

You are a gift to the world, and let your light shine, let it become light.

CHAPTER

A NEW BEGINNING

When the student is ready, the teacher appears.

Right now, we are living in a time where a global pandemic is affecting the entire human race, forcing everyone into isolation. At this moment, I am completing my second book, which I have written with great passion and love, to help as many people as possible awaken. My goal is to remind them of what they may have forgotten, and for them to realize that they are the creators of the reality they live in according to the laws of this universe. By understanding and applying these laws, they can create whatever they desire.

I know that many people have seen this pandemic as something negative. Life here on this planet has taken its toll. People have begun to lose their connection with themselves, and now, nature has acted. This is a shared manifestation. It overcomes the fear of the collective consciousness, just as when I was sick and didn't like it, I played the victim and didn't want to admit that I manifested the illness myself and reached rock bottom.

Today, I tell people that everything happens for us, not against us. I know that for some, it may be hard to believe, just as I didn't want to believe that what happened to me was for my awakening-to realize who I truly am.

The pandemic is waking up the masses because many have been lost in the illusion of the ego. Now is the time, as I explained in Ram Dass's perspective, for transformation. Never before have there been so many spiritual teachers, those who have come with the mission to help others awaken. Some might say they don't need anyone and that they can achieve it on their own. But we are not separate. Separation does not exist. I explained this through universal laws, and through you and me, God is manifested. He is everywhere, in all things. And you can only truly see this after a long period of meditation.

Much of what you have read in this book you have not heard in school or from your family. All people see the world through the lenses they wear, and I believe, through the filters they hold, from their life experiences. My truth does not need to be yours; that is your freedom to choose what to believe. I have opened up, I have come out of the things I thought were the way they were. A wise saying goes: "Everyone is right in their own way," and it's true because everyone sees life the way they are, and they want to convince others that this is the truth. This is how much energy is expended each day in trying to make someone believe it, and if they believe it, it becomes their reality. You can choose what you want to take on.

You can start a new life, create your best version, and with this book, you have not come across it by chance, to begin a new beginning. Let every challenge be a teacher for you. Everyone who comes into your life and every problem is an opportunity to rise higher. If you don't take steps in the direction of becoming the person you want to be, one day you will get there. The first step is the most important. I tell you that there is no one who cannot develop their mind, happiness, vitality, and live a joyful life. And you can do this by rising, growing, little by little, taking responsibility for your life, changing your habits and beliefs. Your life will begin to blossom like a flower, and it will start to bloom.

Our hearts know only one truth, and this truth, sooner or later, each person will recognize when they are ready to open up to the love from which we were born. Start believing that your heart knows the way, and it will guide you through a sense of lightness, through joy, through peace. He who follows their heart is a light for the world, showing others the way, as a fulfilled and happy person. If we open our hearts to forgive, to love, to believe, and follow our inner guidance, we will begin to bloom and uncover the infinite beauty within us.

Embrace yourself and accept all that you have experienced as a gift, so that today you can start your journey from a new beginning. Accept yourself and start being your best friend, focused on yourself. When you are in harmony with yourself and do not betray your feelings, then energy flows freely through your body. Forgive all those who did not know any better because everyone reacts and acts based on what they know. And all the emotional pain you have experienced can be turned into gold, and you can create a wonderful life.

Open your heart for love, for yourself, and for life!

Each person is unique and carries with them gifts for the world through their actions and service. Everyone has a mission here on Earth. The heart shows you the way to discover the gifts you will use to serve life.

CHAPTER

My Journey to My True Self

Me and Me

Who am I? This question followed me for several years: who am I really? The journey to discovering this began with the first step, to uncover and feel who I truly am deep inside. A desire, a will, ignited within me to follow this path. Pain led me on this journey-my emotional pain-and from that inner impulse, I knew deep down that there was more to me than what I had been consciously aware of.

Nothing comes into our lives unless we are ready to receive it, and so I continued my journey toward my true self. I know that for those at the beginning of their spiritual journey, this may sound strange, but those things you have read, the things you have already encountered, are things you now know; they have awakened something in you, perhaps a question of who you truly are.

For many years, I thought I had only one self, the one I identified with as Valentina, the sister, the mother, the wife, and so on. And I was my problems, the emotional pain I carried within me, and I identified myself as being exactly that. Perhaps you've asked yourself the same question at times, because intuitively you know that you are not your ego. Through meditation and time spent confronting everything I had buried in my subconscious, with acceptance of everything, I lovingly embraced all the pain I had experienced, and once again, I released the blockages that had accumulated in me. It was a process of opening my eyes, though I didn't want to see certain situations, because the pain needed to be fully felt to be released. Through the release of everything, I began to feel more at peace and connected with love.

Within me, I healed my inner child through awareness, meditation, and a deeper understanding. As I confronted everything, energy began to naturally flow through me. I am trying to explain the moment when I felt harmony in my body. It is an indescribable feeling. I entered the field of cosmic energy, connected with my higher self, and tuned into the frequency of God. For many people, this might seem like a dream or a fantasy, but it is something everyone can achieve. There, I felt that I have no gender, no name, no role, no form, no body-I simply am.

At first, I didn't know how to explain what had happened, nor did I know what I had experienced, so I began to read many books, and none of them came to me by chance. From that moment on, I understood that everything I had thought I was, was merely a desire to be happy, and through releasing all my fears, I became whole and fulfilled.

If I could explain it in two words, but as many before me and today from those who have reached it, it cannot be explained; it will be achieved. And nothing is impossible for me. I had the courage to step out and give others the impulse to bring them closer to this, to show them that there is more than what we think we are, to remind them of what we truly are. What we are cannot be extinguished, age, or die. All those things I heard for years, such as success, wealth, and fame, were no longer important to me. It felt like I had achieved everything, and I felt no sense of lack.

In that moment, I experienced something wonderful. I saw who I truly was, but I had no clear idea why I was here, why that other version of me had chosen to be here, in this time, in this place, in this life. What is the meaning of my coming here? What is it that I need to give to the world? What is my gift to the world?

Through these words, I want you to feel the energy with which I have written this book. The feeling of passion for life within me, the love for you, for life, for myself. Also, a source from within, naturally and with intelligence, with everything I have gathered over the years, I want to tell you that what you think you are is very small compared to what you truly are. Believe that there is more; it is a field where you can connect with all the information, with all the wisdom that exists, and you have it all within yourself.

I am very grateful for the journey I have taken, and I want to tell you that on the other side of the river, there is a life where you can be happy, at peace, and in harmony with yourself. I have believed and walked this path. I trusted those who showed me the way, and I just kept walking. I wanted to feel it and experience it myself, and today I am here among you as a collective manifestation, a manifestation of yours to give you a sign, an impulse to begin this journey and create the life you want.

Use the universal laws for a more beautiful, easier life on this planet. The love of God is shown through service, and this is my mission: to serve you, to be here for you, so that together we can live in harmony with these laws and see each other as something magnificent. Because we are divine love, we are spirit, a manifestation of God who, through us, manifests every day. Embrace the truth that we are one. And when we understand this, we know that God is in everyone and in us.

I am here.

I am here, you cannot see me,
I am the light that makes you beautiful
You cannot hear me, I speak through your voice
You cannot feel me, I am the strength of your hands
I work, even though my paths are not understood
I work, even though you don't see my works
I am not a supernatural creation, I am not a mystery
Only in complete inner silence, beyond anything personal, can you know who I am, and only as a feeling and trust
I am here, I listen, I respond
When you need me, I am here
Even when you deny me, I am here
Even when you feel completely abandoned, I am here
In your fears, I am here
In your struggles, I am here
I am here when you pray and when you don't pray
I am in you, and you are in me
Only in your consciousness can you feel separated from me
But only in your consciousness can you know and experience me
Free your fear of foolishness from your heart
If you don't walk the path with yourself, I am here
You yourself cannot do it, but I can do everything, and I am in everything
Even if the good doesn't please you, the good is here, I am the good
I am here because I must be, because I am
Only in me does the world have meaning

A New Beginning

Only from me does the world take shape
I am the law that moves everything and grows all things, I nourish them.
I am love, and it is fulfillment. I am security, I am peace
I am unity
I am the law by which you can live
I am your security, I am your peace
I am one with you, I am
Even if you fail to seek me, I do not fail you
Even though your trust in me is uncertain, my trust in you never wavers,
because I know you. Because I love you
I love you, I am here.

(James Dillet Freeman)

www.ingramcontent.com/pod-product-compliance
Lightning Source LLC
Chambersburg PA
CBHW071755120626
46550CB00002B/800

* 9 7 8 1 9 8 8 6 8 0 9 0 3 *